Praise for
me and white supremacy

"America needed this book yesterday. In fact, America has always needed this book. Layla Saad is one of the most important and valuable teachers we have right now on the subject of white supremacy and racial injustice. With keen intelligence and tireless patience, she is working to remove our collective cultural blind spots and to help—at last—change minds and transform society. I have the deepest respect for her. Buy this book for yourself, your family, your students. Don't put it off and don't look away. It's time."

ELIZABETH GILBERT, *New York Times* **bestselling author**

"Layla F. Saad's *Me and White Supremacy* teaches readers exactly how to get past the paralysis of white fragility so that they can build bridges, not walls."

SOPHIA BUSH, award-winning actress and activist

"The book of a lifetime that will transform lives."

REEMA ZAMAN, award-winning actress, speaker, activist, and author of *I Am Yours*

"I suspect that as a result of *Me and White Supremacy*, we will never be the same."

EBONYJANICE MOORE, author, activist, scholar, and founder of Black Girl Mixtape Institute

"This book is a revolution that will create ripples and waves for an entire generation of truth-seekers."

REBEKAH BORUCKI, bestselling author of *Managing the Motherload*

"Layla Saad is an unapologetic force against white supremacy."

JASMIN KAUR, author of *When You Ask Me Where I'm Going*

"*Me and White Supremacy* summons forth a new type of leadership and accountability that this time so desperately calls for and is the pathway to a greater healing that generations of people and communities so desperately need."

LATHAM THOMAS, author of *Own Your Glow* and founder of Mama Glow

ME AND WHITE SUPREMACY

YOUNG READERS' EDITION

LAYLA F. SAAD

This work is adapted for young readers and is based on *Me and White Supremacy: Combat Racism, Change the World, and Become a Good Ancestor* by Layla F. Saad, copyright © 2020 by Layla F. Saad, published by Sourcebooks.

Sourcebooks eXplore and the colophon are registered trademarks of Sourcebooks.

This publication is designed to provide accurate and authoritative information in regard to the subject matter covered. It is sold with the understanding that the publisher is not engaged in rendering legal, accounting, or other professional service. If legal advice or other expert assistance is required, the services of a competent professional person should be sought.
—*From a Declaration of Principles Jointly Adopted by a Committee of the American Bar Association and a Committee of Publishers and Associations*

Published by Sourcebooks eXplore, an imprint of Sourcebooks Kids
P.O. Box 4410, Naperville, Illinois 60567–4410
(630) 961-3900
sourcebookskids.com

Library of Congress Cataloging-in-Publication Data is on file with the publisher.

Source of Production: Versa Press, East Peoria, Illinois, United States
Date of Production: December 2021
Run Number: 5024094

Printed and bound in the United States of America.
VP 10 9 8 7 6 5 4 3 2 1

contents

welcome letter from the author

Dear Reader,

Welcome!

My name is Layla Saad, and I'm going to be guiding you on a journey to help you explore and understand racism and white supremacy and how you can help change the world.

But first of all, I want to start by asking you how you felt when you first saw the title of this book. Were you curious? Intrigued? Confused? Uncomfortable? Maybe all of the above? I want to reassure you that all those feelings and more are completely normal. This is a challenging book, but it is also a hopeful one.

In chapter 4, I'm going to explain more about what *white supremacy* is. But before we go any further, I'm going to give you a brief explanation so that you understand what this book is about.

White supremacy is a racist ideology that is based on the belief that white people are superior to and better than people of other races, and therefore they deserve to be dominant over and treated better than people of other races.

This idea probably feels wrong and unfair to you, and it is. All people should be treated equally no matter their skin color. Unfortunately, the world we live in today is not always a fair place, and white supremacy has been embedded in our lives for hundreds of years. And unless we do something about it, it will continue to be embedded in our lives for hundreds of years to come. And that's why I wrote this book. To help you understand what white supremacy is, how it works, and how you can help dismantle it so that we can create a fairer world.

Talking about white supremacy is often a challenging subject for young people and adults alike. So whatever emotions you are feeling right now or throughout this book are completely okay. Over the course of this journey, I am going to do my very best to help guide you through this topic in a way that makes it easy for you to understand these issues, how they impact your life and the lives of other people around you, and what you can do to help create an antiracist world where people of all races are treated with respect, dignity, and equality. Antiracism is how we actively work toward creating a world without racism.

My hope is that when you finish this book, you will feel a lot more comfortable and confident talking about white supremacy and antiracism. My aim throughout this journey is to give you the knowledge and tools you need to help change the world.

This book is a young readers' edition of a book that was first written for adults called *Me and White Supremacy: Combat Racism, Change the World, and Become a Good Ancestor*. In that book, I was specifically talking to adults who were white or who had white privilege (more on this in chapter 5). In this book, however, I'm talking to readers of *all* races. That's because I believe it is important for all young people to understand these topics so that you can grow into adults who know how to have conversations about race and racism with confidence and know how to work together collectively to create an antiracist world.

This is a book that you can read alone or with others. You might be reading this book by yourself, with your class or club, or with family or friends. As I'll explain a little later, this isn't only a book that you *read*, it's also a book that you *do*. In each of the chapters in part 2, I've included some reflection questions for you to help take the learning even deeper. Feel free to use these questions to journal with or to discuss with others. The more you interact with these reflection questions, the more you will get out of this book.

Lastly, as you go through this book and the reflection questions, you will experience a range of challenging emotions like sadness, anger, frustration, and disgust. I want you to know that as difficult as those emotions are, they are normal and an important part of the work of antiracism. We will talk more about how to process these emotions in chapter 11. Throughout time, white supremacy has harmed people who are not white in the most painful ways. In order to change the world, we need to look at white supremacy throughout history and in our lives and the lives of people around us today. And that is really hard to do. But I believe that it is the work that we *must* do. And I believe it is work that we *can* do. However, please know that it is also important for us to focus on more positive emotions like love, hope, and compassion in our antiracism work. We can work together joyfully to create a better world.

I want you to know that you are not alone on this journey. Adults and young people all over the world are on this same journey with you, and together, we are doing important work. There are change makers from around the world who have dedicated themselves to fighting racism and creating an antiracist world. You can become one of those change makers too.

You can help change the world. Let's begin now.

PART I

introduction

CHAPTER 1

how to use this book

Here are some tips for reading this book, whether you are reading it alone or with others.

KEEP A JOURNAL

This is a book that is designed not just to be read but also to be worked through. The best way to do that is to use a special journal to answer the reflection questions in the chapters. This journal can then become your antiracism journal, which you can refer back to anytime.

GO AT YOUR OWN PACE

We cover a lot of things in this book that may be new to you and may be challenging for you to think about and discuss. There's no need to rush through the book; you can go as slow or as fast as you are comfortable. Remember it's not a competition; it's a journey.

RECAP, REFLECT, RESPOND

Throughout the book, I've tried to share as much as I can to help you understand how white supremacy operates and how we can work to dismantle it within ourselves and our communities. In part 2, each chapter covers a different aspect of white supremacy, and all the chapters follow the same format. For example, our first chapter in part 2 on white privilege is outlined as follows:

❖ *What is white privilege?* We explore what it is using personal stories, history, pop culture, and the media.

❖ *How does white privilege show up?* We examine examples of what it looks like in practice.

❖ *Why do we need to look at white privilege?* We discuss why it's important for us to understand how it relates to white supremacy and racism.

❖ *Recap, reflect, respond.* We recap the definition, answer some reflective questions, and explore ways to practice antiracism in our lives. In some chapters, the reflect and respond sections have different questions and advice for people who have white privilege versus those who don't have white privilege. That's because depending on our race, our way of practicing antiracism often can and will look different.

ADVICE FOR READING WITH A GROUP

You can use this book alone or read it with a group of other people who are also seeking to practice antiracism. For those reading with a group, you may be using this book with your family, your friends, your community interest group, or at school. Here are some basic guidelines for how to read this book in a group:

❖ Read the chapters together, or read alone and then discuss the chapters together. You can use the reflection questions in each chapter for your discussions.

❖ Have a consistent schedule for when you are going to meet to discuss the book, for example every

Monday at 1:00 p.m. in class or every Sunday at 5:00 p.m. at home.

❖ Make sure your group is nonhierarchical, meaning make sure it's a group where everybody's voice is valued and listened to. Don't talk over one another or allow one or two people's voices to dominate the discussion. A suggestion is to have guidelines that say in order to talk, you must raise your hand or hold a talking stick, and only one person can talk at a time. Another helpful suggestion is to go around in a circle to make sure each person's voice is heard.

❖ Sometimes it's good to take breaks in between discussions when things are getting a bit heavy. Make sure everyone knows that they can call for a break if they need one. You could even schedule a half-time break so that people can have a time-out from the challenging conversations.

❖ It's okay and important for people to express their emotions while reading the book. As we will discuss in chapter 11, it's normal to experience a range of different feelings while reading this book and learning about white supremacy. It's also okay to disagree and to have different perspectives. Remember, everyone has their own identities and experiences, so we are not always going to agree on everything! That's totally okay. However, do make sure that you stay respectful, kind, and compassionate to one another at all times. Practicing antiracism means treating others the way we would like to be treated. As we explore in chapter 18, we don't have to cancel one another if we mess up or have disagreements.

❖ If an adult is leading your group, ask them to first work through the adult version of *Me and White Supremacy* and to review the appendix of that book, which lays out a process called the Circle Way, which is helpful for leading Me and White Supremacy Reading Circles.

❖ Know that this book was written for people of all races to explore their relationship with white supremacy and learn how they can practice antiracism. It's important that everyone in the group participate equally, and that an expectation should not be placed on the people of color in the group to answer all the questions about race and racism that the white people in the group may have. Instead, I encourage you to explore together, sharing your own experiences, and respectfully asking questions that can take your understanding deeper.

CHAPTER 2

a little about me!

As we are going to be spending quite some time together on this journey, I think it's important for you to know a little about me—your guide—before we begin.

My name is Layla Saad, and I am an author who writes about race, identity, leadership, personal transformation, and social change. I am extremely passionate about doing work that helps to positively change people's lives and makes the world a better place for people of all races.

The first thing to know about me is that I hold a few different identities and experiences at the same time. I am an East African, Middle Eastern, Black, British,

Muslim woman. I live in Qatar, and I speak with, write to, and teach people all over the world. I am a third-culture kid, which is a person who was raised in a culture that is different from the culture of their parents or the culture of their country of nationality.

My mother was born and grew up in Zanzibar and my father in Kenya. As young adults, they immigrated to the United Kingdom, where they met each other and got married. My two younger brothers and I were born and spent the early years of our childhood in Wales. We lived for a short while in Tanzania with my mother's family, and then we moved to England for a number of years, and then onward to Qatar, where I still live today with my husband and our two children, Maya and Mohamed, and our two cats, Oreo and Marshmallow.

When I was growing up, I thought that being a third-culture kid made me weird or wrong because I never felt like I really fit in. However, what I've come to understand and love about being a third-culture kid is that I can talk to and relate with anyone around the world—especially others who also feel like they don't fit in. As an adult, I see that my identities and experiences as a third-culture kid are among my superpowers. But as a kid, I didn't really understand that.

You see, I spent the first part of my childhood, between the ages of three and fifteen years old, going to schools in the UK that were predominantly white and Christian. I was always the only Black and Muslim girl in all my classes, and I had no friends who I could talk to about what it felt like to be Black in largely white spaces. A lot of the time, I felt odd, weird, different, and wrong. I just wanted to be treated like everyone else.

The one thing that made a huge positive difference in how I saw myself was that I grew up with amazing parents who affirmed our cultural identities. My father spent his career sailing around the world as a mariner. He would travel to far-off places and bring us back gifts and stories from other countries. He instilled in my brothers and me a philosophy of being "citizens of the world." This idea that there is nowhere in the world where we do not belong—and that we don't have to fit into anyone else's ideas of who they think we should be—has stayed with me to this day. My mother took on the huge task of raising my siblings and me alone during the long months when my father was working at sea. She was dedicated to creating an environment in our home where our cultural identity and our religious beliefs were nurtured and practiced. My mother spoke to us in both English and Swahili (my parents' mother tongue) and taught us about Islam and how to practice our religion. The loving foundation she laid in those years of our childhood still stands strong today. When I was at home, I never felt that there was anything wrong with being a Black Muslim girl.

But every time I left the house, every time I went to school, every time I watched TV, every time I connected with the rest of the world, I was interacting with white supremacy. Every day, in little and not-so-little ways, I was reminded that I was "other" or different—and not in a good way. That I was less than people who were white.

I didn't have many incidents where I experienced overt racism such as someone calling me a racist word. But in countless subtle ways, every day, I experienced racism indirectly. And those indirect messages—from being treated slightly differently by schoolteachers, to hardly ever seeing fictional characters or media representations that looked like me, to understanding that I would have to work a lot harder than my white friends to be treated the same as them—painted an unforgettable picture in my mind. A picture that taught me this: Black girls like me did not matter in a white world. I will spend the rest of my life tearing down this picture and

painting a new one that reflects the truth: Black girls—
and Black people—matter. Everywhere.

Across my lifetime, I have lived on three different
continents: Europe, Africa, and Asia. I have spent just
over half that time living outside the Western world, but
that does not mean that the effects of white supremacy
have not continued to impact me. As you will come to
understand as we travel on this journey, white supremacy harms Black people, Indigenous people, and People
of Color (the acronym we'll be using for this is BIPOC)
all around the world in different ways—in person,
online, and in the media. I do the work that I do to stop
this harm and to help create a better world.

My work is born out of both the pain and the pride
of being a Black child and a Black woman. It is painful
to me to know how BIPOC like me are seen and treated
because of the color of our skin. At the same time, I feel
incredibly proud to stand in the fullness of who I am as
a Black woman and to support other BIPOC to do the
same for themselves too.

I do this work because white supremacy negatively
impacted how I saw myself when I was young and
how the world still sees and treats me today. I do this
work because white supremacy will negatively impact

my children and my children's children. I do this work because it hurts me that Black people around the world are treated as inferior because of the color of our skin. I do this work because BIPOC everywhere deserve to be treated with dignity and respect, something that white supremacy strips us of. I do this work because I have a voice, and it is my responsibility to use my voice to dismantle a system that has hurt me and that hurts BIPOC every day. I do this work because I was called to it, and I answered that call.

The concepts that I have brought together in this book begin from my own personal lived experiences. They are deepened and further illustrated by drawing on examples from experiences I have witnessed, historical contexts, cultural moments, fictional and nonfictional literature, the media, and more.

It is my intention that this work—which is a combination of learning and reflective questions—will create a deep shift in thinking and action within you to help create a world without white supremacy. A world where everybody, of every race, feels safe and lives free. My hope is that this book will give you the tools you need to help become an antiracist change maker.

CHAPTER 3

a little about you!

Recognizing and owning our identities is an important part of understanding how to practice antiracism. White supremacy exists to benefit people who are white or who look white and to oppress or harm people who are not white or who don't look white. For that reason, the roles and responsibilities we have in dismantling it and practicing antiracism are different depending on our identities.

If you are white or appear to others to be white, white supremacy gives you certain benefits and privileges that make your life safer. People generally treat you better, and you generally *don't* experience racism, discrimination, or oppression because of your race.

If you are Black, Indigenous, or a Person of Color who doesn't look white, white supremacy doesn't give you any benefits or privileges that make your life safer. People generally treat you as lesser than, and you generally *do* experience racism, discrimination, and oppression because of your race.

If you are biracial or multiracial or a Person of Color who may pass as white to others, depending on how close to white or black or brown your skin color is, white supremacy impacts you in ways where sometimes you *do* experience certain benefits and privileges, and sometimes you *don't*, and instead you *do* experience racism, discrimination, and oppression because of your race. People sometimes treat you better and sometimes treat you as lesser than, depending on the circumstances.

You may have heard the words *race*, *ethnicity*, and *nationality*. These three identities mean three distinct things and are not interchangeable with one another. The definitions of these words are a little tricky to understand sometimes, but understanding them is an important part of this journey.

UNDERSTANDING RACE, ETHNICITY, AND NATIONALITY

❖ **RACE:** Refers to a grouping of humans based on shared observable, physical features, such as skin color, facial features, and hair textures. Examples of different races include Black, white, Asian, Native American, and others.

❖ **ETHNICITY:** Refers to a grouping of humans based on shared social traits, such as language, ancestry, history, place of origin, or culture. Examples of different ethnicities include Arab, Jewish, English, Dutch, Korean, Chinese, Nigerian, Tanzanian, Mexican, Māori, and others.

❖ **NATIONALITY:** Refers to your country of citizenship, the country on your passport or where you hold legal rights as a citizen. Examples of different nationalities include British, American, Kenyan, French, Australian, Argentinian, and others.

When I shared a little about me, the first thing I shared with you were my racial, ethnic, and national identities as well as my religion and where I live.

❖ **WHO AM I?** I am an East African, Middle Eastern, Black, British, Muslim woman who lives in Qatar.

- ❖ **WHAT IS MY RACE?** I identify as Black.
- ❖ **WHAT IS MY ETHNICITY?** East African and Middle Eastern.
- ❖ **WHAT IS MY NATIONALITY?** British. Although I live in Qatar, I was born in the United Kingdom and am a UK citizen and passport holder.

Some of these are very broad terms, so I'd like to break them down a little bit more. My mother's ethnicities include Zanzibari, Omani, and (according to my maternal grandmother) Iranian. My father's ethnicities include Kenyan (including Maasai and Kikuyu tribes), Tanzanian, and probably Comoro Islands and Yemeni (according to family elders).

Because of historical emigration and colonization, my family may have other unknown ethnicities that we are unaware of that go a few more centuries back. However, broadly speaking, both of my parents belong to the ethnic and cultural group called Swahili people, who inhabit East Africa and speak Swahili, as well as the Arab people of the Arabian Gulf from the country of Oman, who speak Arabic.

My spoken languages are English, a bit of Swahili, and a little bit of Arabic. Our religion is Islam (a religion practiced by many—but not all—people across East

Africa and the Middle East). And our cultural foods, holidays, traditions, and practices are a reflection of our ethnicity and religion.

I have a lot of different parts of identity that make up part of who I am. My race, ethnicity, and nationality tell you a lot about me but not everything! There are other parts of my identity that are equally important in understanding who I am, such as my gender, my age, my physical ability, my likes and dislikes, my personality, my favorite hobbies, and my life experiences. As human beings, we are complex and interesting, and no one is like anyone else.

In this book, we are mainly focusing on the identities of race and ethnicity, because that is where white supremacy affects us. Even though our racial and ethnic identities only make up part of who we are, our experiences of life are often very different depending on what those identities are. As a Black person, I experience racism, discrimination, and oppression because of white supremacy, because white supremacy says that Black people are inferior to (or lesser than) people who are white. Even though this isn't true and even though being Black is only one part of who I am, white supremacy makes my race define *all* of who I am and then discriminates against me because of it.

We will dive more into race and racism in the next chapter. Before we do that, it's your turn to look at your race, ethnicity, and nationality.

TO HELP YOU, HERE ARE SOME IMPORTANT POINTS TO KEEP IN MIND:

❖ **RACE:** You might identify as one, two, or more races, depending on your family. Biracial people are people whose parents are two different races, such as Black and white. Multiracial people are people whose parents are more than two different races, such as Black, white, and Asian. As you'll find out soon, race is not a fixed thing, and people identify themselves differently. You might have a white parent and a Black parent and identify only as Black or as Black biracial. It also depends on how race is classified in the country you live in.

❖ **ETHNICITY:** You may or may not know what your ethnicity is for various reasons. For example, you may not know your ethnicity if no one in your family has ever talked about ethnicity or knows about their ethnicity. You may not know your exact ethnicity if you are a descendant of ancestors who were enslaved Africans. Another reason you might not know your ethnicity is if you were adopted or orphaned, with no background knowledge of your ethnicity. If you don't know your ethnicity, it's okay! Remember, these identities only make up part of who we are. They don't make up all of who we are. Your family may be able to tell you more about your ethnicity, but if they can't, don't worry.

❖ **NATIONALITY:** Your nationality isn't just about what country your passport is from or what country you are a legal citizen of. It also says a lot about the culture you grew up in, the language you speak, the values you hold, and the place you call home. Although I have a very varied ethnic background, the culture I was born and grew up in was British. The language I speak as my first language is English. Some of the values I have about life are British values, and the UK is one of the places I call home. Even though I am not ethnically Welsh, English, or European, being British is as much a part of who I am as my actual ethnicities.

When we talk about our own or other people's races, ethnicities, and nationalities, we should not try to put people in boxes. Instead, we should try to understand our similarities and differences so that we can better respect them. Understanding race, ethnicity, and nationality can also help us to understand how white supremacy categorizes us into these different boxes and then treats us differently accordingly.

BEFORE WE MOVE ON, HERE ARE SOME QUESTIONS TO REFLECT ON:

1. What race(s) do you identify as?
2. What ethnicity or ethnicities do you hold?
3. What is your nationality?
4. Other than your race, ethnicity, and nationality, who are you? What other important parts of your identity, experiences, personality, likes and dislikes, make up who you are?

WHAT DO YOU ALREADY KNOW?

This book is a journey to help you understand race, racism, and white supremacy. But before we go on that journey, I'd like for you to explore what you already know about these things. We've talked a little already about race, ethnicity, and nationality. Perhaps you learned some things in that section that you didn't really know before or were not entirely sure about. But what *do* you know? What things have you heard your friends, family, classmates, teachers, favorite celebrities, politicians, and people on TV saying about race and racism?

LET'S TAKE A FEW MINUTES TO REFLECT AND JOURNAL:

❖ Before learning about race in this chapter, what did you think the word *race* meant?

❖ What do you think the word *racism* means?

❖ What do you think the term *white supremacy* means?

❖ What conversations have you had with your friends about race? What about racism?

❖ What conversations have you had with your parents and family members about race and racism?

❖ What conversations have your teachers had with you and your classmates about race and racism? Have you ever learned about these things in your school lessons? If so, what did you learn?

❖ Have you ever had any conversations with people in your life about white supremacy?

❖ What things have you heard or seen on TV about race and racism?

❖ Have you ever experienced racism? What happened? How did it make you feel?

❖ Have any of your friends or family ever experienced racism? What happened? How do you think it made them feel?

❖ Have you ever done or said something racist (even if you didn't mean it or didn't know that it was racist)? How did that make you feel? Did you apologize for it?

❖ How does talking about race and racism make you feel? How does talking about your racial identity make you feel?

❖ Do you have any fears or nervousness about doing or saying the wrong thing when it comes to racism?

❖ What questions do you wish you could ask an expert about race or racism?

Great job! Some of those questions may have been a little bit awkward or uncomfortable to answer. Just remember that there are no right or wrong answers. This is just about understanding what you already know. This book is here to help you learn more.

CHAPTER 4

what is white supremacy?

You may have noticed that sometimes I use the word *racism* and sometimes I use the term *white supremacy*. Actually, these two words don't mean the same thing, but they are very much connected.

Racism is the belief that different groupings of people can be divided into some groups that are superior and some that are inferior based on their race or ethnicity. The ones who are grouped as superior are then given more power and privileges, are generally seen as better, and are treated better by society. The ones who are grouped as inferior are given less power and fewer privileges, are generally seen as lesser than, and are discriminated against by society. Racism isn't just about what people believe about different races. It's also about how society is structured to give some people advantages because of their race and other people disadvantages because of their race.

White supremacy is a type of racism. It is based on the racist idea that white people are superior to people of *all* other races and therefore should be dominant over and treated better than people of *all* other races. When I talk about racism in this book, I am talking specifically about white supremacy racism.

There are many different types of racism that exist in different parts of the world and throughout history. However white supremacy is the racism that has had the biggest impact on our entire modern world. To understand why that is, we need to take a little trip through history to understand where the ideas of race, racism, and white supremacy that we know today come from and how they have shaped our world.

HISTORY TRIP: THERE'S NO SUCH THING AS RACE...OR IS THERE?

In the last chapter, I talked about race, ethnicity, and nationality. I defined race as a grouping of humans based on shared observable, physical features, such as skin color, facial features, and hair textures. Examples of different races include Black, white, Asian, Native American, and others.

Actually, there's no such thing as different human races! There is only one race—the human race, or *Homo sapiens*. A huge international scientific research study called the Human Genome Project confirmed this in 2003. Scientists in the Human Genome Project spent thirteen years identifying and mapping human DNA, and one of the major findings of the project was that despite the fact that human beings from different places look different from one another, inside our genes, we are almost entirely the same. In fact, the project showed that there is only about .01 percent difference between people who look racially different. That means that people who look racially different on the outside are actually about 99.99 percent the same on the inside!

So why would we divide people up into different

races and say some races are superior to others when we are almost entirely the same?

THERE ARE TWO REASONS FOR THIS:

1. Centuries ago, when white Europeans were traveling to different parts of the world and coming into contact with non-European people, there was a lot of debate about whether human beings come from one human origin (monogenism) or whether we come from different human origins (polygenism). People at the time didn't know the answer to this question, and modern science hadn't yet proven that the winner of the debate was monogenism. Polygenism was the popular theory at the time, and scientists in those days spent a lot of time speculating and writing about the idea of different races having different characteristics.

2. Polygenism and the idea of different races were used to justify colonialism, land theft, and enslavement by white European people over non-European people.

There were many different European thinkers in the seventeenth to nineteenth centuries who wrote books and shared their ideas about race. They did not just describe what different people of different races looked like, but they also ascribed untrue behavioral characteristics to each race, putting them in categories where some races were more beautiful, intelligent, moral, and desirable than other races. According to all these thinkers, the race that was the best race of all races was the white or European race. And often, the race that was described as the worst of all races was the Black or African race. For example, the eighteenth-century German philosopher Christoph Meiners split humankind into two main divisions and called them "the beautiful white race" and "the ugly black race."

> These ideas are where the roots of white supremacy begin, in this idea that white people are the most *supreme* people of all people in the world.

One of the most famous of these theorists was Carl Linnaeus. Linnaeus was a Swedish botanist, physician, and zoologist who wrote a book called *Systema Naturae* in the eighteenth century. This book divided people into four main categories and is where we first see people being referred to using colors.

These categories were Americanus (also called

red), Europaeus (also called white), Asiaticus (also called yellow), and Africanus (also called black). Linnaeus ascribed different stereotyped behaviors to each category. For example, Americanus or Native people were described as stubborn and zealous. Asiaticus people were described as haughty and greedy. Africanus people were described as sly, lazy, and crafty. But Europaeus people were described as gentle and inventive.

Do you notice a trend here? People who were not white were described in stereotypically negative ways, but people who were white were described in stereotypically positive ways (we'll talk more about racist stereotypes in chapter 14).

Later thinkers also continued to share similar racist beliefs. Thomas Jefferson, one of the founding fathers of the United States of America, believed that Black people were "inferior to the whites in the endowments of body and mind."

Georges Cuvier, an eighteenth-century French naturalist and zoologist, wrote that "the white race, with oval face, straight hair and nose, to which the civilized people of Europe belong and which appear to us the most beautiful of all, is also superior to others by its genius, courage, and activity." Cuvier also believed that Black people had the smallest brains of all the races.

Franz Ignaz Pruner, a nineteenth-century German physician, ophthalmologist, and anthropologist, claimed that Black people had brains very similar to those of apes and that they had a shortened big toe that connected them closely to apes.

> These theories and ideas sound ridiculous today, but at the time, they were treated as scientific facts and are what we call **scientific racism**.

Scientific racism was used as a way to explain that people who were not white were not full human beings in the same way that white people were. Black people were seen as being scientifically more like animals than humans. And people of other races were seen as scientifically lesser human beings who were not as civilized, smart, powerful, or whole as white people.

Today we know that there is no such thing as scientific differences in people of different colors, cultures, and ethnicities. We know that being white doesn't scientifically make you more beautiful or smart, and being

Black doesn't make you scientifically less intelligent or less human. We know that scientifically, our skin color has nothing to do with our abilities, our worth, or our humanity. The theory of different human races is not a scientific or biological fact.

HOWEVER, WE STILL REFER TO PEOPLE AS DIFFERENT RACES. WHY IS THAT?

It's because even though the biological idea of race isn't real, the social idea of race *is* real. "Social" means created by human beings (rather than based on scientific facts). Throughout history and today, society categorizes people in different ways depending on how they look, primarily the color of their skin. And then it gives or denies these "races" different societal privileges and causes them to have very different experiences.

For example, even though there is biologically only one race, Black people in the United States are more likely to be criminalized than white people. This isn't because white people commit less crime (they don't!). Instead, it's a combination of racist factors including the fact that Black people are often stereotyped in negative ways to make them seem more criminal. Remember Linnaeus's description of Black people as being sly and

crafty? Even though this has been proven to be scientifically untrue, people still unconsciously hold these
stereotypes and use them to justify criminalizing Black
people more than white people.

> It's important to understand that the idea
> of race was also created to justify racism.

When ideas of different races were created centuries
ago, they were not just about classifying people for scientific reasons. They were about classifying people for
power reasons. If one group could be defined as more
"superior" than another, then it was seen as okay that
the "inferior" group was given less power, freedom, and
rights. European people used this idea to justify stealing
land, resources, and even people from non-European
places, and it was deemed correct for white people to
suppress and oppress nonwhite people. This is why the
social idea of race is still upheld today, because it justi-
fies why some people are given more power and privileges than other people.

> Race is also a social idea because the concept
> of who is white has changed over time.

At one time, Irish people were not considered white in the United States. Currently in the United States, Middle Eastern and North African people are classified as white, even though they are not of European descent. In the early twentieth century, visibly white people in the United States were classified as Black if even one of their ancestors was Black. This was called the one-drop rule. The rule didn't apply the other way around though—if Black people had one ancestor who was white, they were not classed as white. The social idea of race comes in part from scientific racism and is used as a way to grant power and privileges to white people and deny these things to people of other races.

> The social idea of race is also the way that many people connect with each other through their shared experiences of having the same skin color.

This way of connecting with each other can be positive or negative. For example, white nationalists connect with each other over their belief that being white makes them superior to everyone else. They only want to be around other white people and do not want people of other races to be in relationships with them or even live in the same places they do. On the other hand, Black people around the world (also called the African diaspora) often connect with each other over their shared cultural experiences of being of African descent and knowing what it is like to be on the receiving end of anti-Black racism. This way of connecting isn't about excluding other races but is instead about celebrating similarities and shared experiences.

We'll talk more about racial color blindness and the idea of "seeing race" in chapter 12.

FOR NOW, THE TWO IMPORTANT THINGS TO UNDERSTAND ARE THESE:

1. While race isn't a biological fact, it is a social fact, and it isn't one that we can ignore if we want to end racism.

2. Racism created race, and not the other way around. White supremacy and racism arose from European people categorizing people into different races using racist ideas of white people being superior or supreme and Black, Brown, and Indigenous people being inferior or lesser than. We can't end racism by pretending that the social

idea of race isn't real. We end racism by bringing an end to the unjust treatment of people who are not white.

That was quite a history trip!

I know we've covered a lot so far on the origins of race, racism, and white supremacy. But to fully understand what white supremacy is, we also have to explore the history of European colonialism and how it created the world that we live in today. Let's take one more history trip before we move on.

HISTORY TRIP: HOW EUROPEAN COLONIALISM SHAPED THE WORLD AND SPREAD GLOBAL WHITE SUPREMACY

Centuries ago, the world wasn't as connected as it is today. Because of the lack of modern technology, people from different countries didn't easily travel across the ocean to other continents. While shorter ship journeys for trade to nearby countries were made by sea, journeys across the ocean were dangerous and expensive.

However, when the Ottoman Empire took control

of Constantinople in 1453, many trade routes to India and China for spices and silk were blocked. As a result, Europeans began to seek their own alternative routes for these goods, and in the fifteenth to eighteenth centuries, they made extensive overseas travels to explore the rest of the world and establish new trade routes so that they could make money.

This was often called the age of discovery or age of exploration, and it marked a time when the Portuguese and Spanish, and later the English, Dutch, French, and Germans, made expeditions to Africa, the Americas, and Asia in search of trading goods, gold, and the acquisition of land.

While this time in history is often described as the age of discovery, the important thing to remember is that these lands were already inhabited by people who had lived there for thousands of years. The Italian explorer Christopher Columbus didn't "discover" America. These lands already existed, and Native Americans had been living there for tens of thousands of years. The lands that Europeans traveled to across Africa, the Americas, and Asia held societies that were thousands of generations old. These societies were highly sophisticated and rich in history, languages, technology, arts, scientific and mathematical knowledge, religion, wealth, architecture, and governance. They also had their own realities of wars, tribal divisions, empires, and enslavement. They had their own thriving and complex existences before the Europeans "discovered" them. The age of discovery marked the beginning of European colonialism, which shaped the modern world, as well as the rise of global white supremacy, which we still live with today.

The impact of European colonization was huge. Millions of Indigenous people around the world were displaced from their lands, killed through diseases and wars, kidnapped and enslaved to work for their oppressors, punished for speaking their native languages and worshipping their own gods, and treated like lower-class beings. They were systematically and purposely stripped of their rights and dignities as white supremacy took over their societies.

Though we are now many centuries into the future and the world has changed immensely, much has also stayed the same. In Western societies and countries with large white populations, white people generally continue to hold certain privileges (we'll explore this more in chapter 5), and BIPOC generally continue to experience personal and systemic racism, discrimination, and the aftereffects of colonization and enslavement. White supremacy continues to shape our world today.

UNDERSTANDING THE FOUR LEVELS OF RACISM

According to Race Forward, a center for racial justice innovation, there are four levels of racism.

1. **INTERNALIZED RACISM:** Also called personal racism, this racism lies *within individuals* and comprises our private and often subconscious beliefs and biases about race and racism, influenced by our culture. This can look like prejudice against people of a different race. For BIPOC, it can look like prejudice against oneself and other BIPOC. For white people, it can look like believing in the superiority of themselves and other white people.

2. **INTERPERSONAL RACISM:** This racism occurs *between individuals*. This is the racism that we see happening between people, whether in the classroom, on the playground, in public, or in the media. For example, tone policing (chapter 7) is a type of interpersonal racism.

3. **INSTITUTIONAL RACISM:** This racism occurs *within institutions and systems of power*. This racism

looks like unfair policies and discriminatory practices by institutions (such as schools, workplaces,
banks, and hospitals) that disadvantage BIPOC and
advantage white people.

4. **STRUCTURAL RACISM:** Also called systemic racism,
   this racism occurs *among institutions and across
   society.* It involves many societal factors, like history, culture, ideology, and the interactions of institutions and policies that disadvantage BIPOC and
   privilege white people.

In this book, we are largely going to be exploring the first
two levels, internalized and interpersonal racism, and
briefly touching on the third level, institutional racism.

In order to completely dismantle white supremacy,
we have to understand and approach it on all four levels.
However, internalized and interpersonal racism are the
important foundation that we need to understand and
combat to truly get rid of institutional and structural racism.

As a young person, you don't yet have the power to
fight institutional and structural racism, but you definitely *do* have what it takes to fight the first two levels
of racism.

Let's begin.

PART II

exploring white supremacy

CHAPTER 5

white privilege

I didn't learn the term *white privilege* until I was an adult, but I learned about the concept when I was a little kid.

One afternoon when I was seven years old, my mother sat me down to talk to me about white privilege, or rather my lack of it. I can't remember exactly how we got on to the conversation, but I will never forget these exact words that she said to me: "Layla, because you are Black, because you are Muslim, and because you are a girl, you are going to have to work three times as hard as everyone else around you to get ahead. You have these three things working against you."

My mother wasn't talking about my race, religion, or gender being inherently flawed, but rather she was making me aware of the fact that we live in a society that treats people who are Black, Muslim, and female in lesser ways than those who are white, Christian, and male. She wanted me to know that I would be treated differently from my friends, who were all white and Christian, and that even though this wasn't fair or right, it was (and still is), sadly, the way things were.

As my mother, she felt that she had to prepare me for a world that would disadvantage me because of my race and advantage white people because of their race. For my protection and survival, she needed me to know that I did not own the privilege of being white in a society and a world that sees white people as superior.

WHAT IS WHITE PRIVILEGE?

Privilege can be defined as a benefit, advantage, or immunity, usually unearned.

Has a parent or adult ever had to talk to you about the disadvantages and dangers you may face in life because of your race? If not, then it's probably because you have white privilege.

White privilege is a term coined by American women's studies scholar Dr. Peggy McIntosh.

HISTORY LESSON

Peggy McIntosh first wrote about white privilege in an article in 1988 called "White Privilege and Male Privilege: A Personal Account of Coming to See Correspondences Through Work in Women's Studies."

She had always been taught that racism was something that disadvantaged people who were not white. But what she had not been taught was that racism was also something that gave her, a white person, certain advantages. She called this an *invisible knapsack*. She wrote, **"I have come to see white privilege as an invisible package of unearned assets that I can count on cashing in each day, but about which I was 'meant' to remain oblivious."**

WHAT DOES THIS MEAN? LET'S BREAK IT DOWN!

- *"an invisible package"*: White privilege isn't an object that we can see or hold, but it exists as something that white people and people who look white carry around with them every day.

- *"of unearned assets"*: White privilege isn't something that white people earn by working hard, paying money, or doing a special task. It is something that our current society gives white people from the moment they are born, simply because they are white or look white.

- *"that I can count on cashing in each day"*: People who are white or look white can use these unearned advantages every day in various different ways, even if they are not trying to.

- *"but about which I was 'meant' to remain oblivious"*: People who are white or look white are not meant to know that they have this privilege. BIPOC know that white people have this privilege, but white people do not know about it themselves. I believe that the reason white people are not meant to know about their white privilege is because if they did, they would probably think it is unfair and try to do something to change it (which is what antiracism is about!).

HOW DOES WHITE PRIVILEGE SHOW UP?

Many of the examples in McIntosh's white privilege checklist are more familiar to adults than to young people. To help you understand this concept better, I've created a white privilege list for you to go through that is more suitable for young people, adapting some of McIntosh's examples and sharing some of my own.

GO THROUGH THE LIST AND NOTE ALL THE EXAMPLES THAT APPLY TO YOU.

❖ I have never been told or felt that others didn't want to play with me or be my friend because of the color of my skin.

❖ I have never been insulted about my race or the color of my skin.

❖ Nobody in my family has ever been insulted or harmed because of their race or the color of their skin.

❖ I have never been asked why my skin is the color that it is.

❖ I have never been asked where I "really" come from.

❖ I have never been told to go back to where I "really" come from. People of my race are never told to go back to where they "really" come from.

❖ I can go to stores alone and not worry about being followed or harassed because of the color of my skin.

❖ I can play outside or hang around outdoors and not worry about being followed, harassed, harmed, or killed because of the color of my skin.

❖ The majority of people on TV shows, in movies, and on the covers of magazines are the same race as me.

❖ In school, when we learn about our country's history or about "civilization," I'm taught that it was made by people who are the same race as me.

❖ My parents do not have to teach me about my race and racism for my daily physical protection.

❖ People don't make assumptions that I am less well-behaved because of the color of my skin.

❖ People don't make assumptions that I am less intelligent because of the color of my skin.

❖ People don't make assumptions that my family has less money because of the color of our skin.

❖ I am never asked to speak for all people of my race (questions like "What do people of your race think about this?")

❖ I can easily find many different types of toys and games featuring people of my race.

- ❖ If I'm having a bad day, it's never been because of something to do with my race.

- ❖ I've never felt or been rejected or excluded because of my race.

- ❖ I never have to worry if my family members are safe because of their race.

- ❖ If I get a cut, I can easily find bandages that closely match my skin color.

- ❖ The majority of leaders in my country are the same race as me.

- ❖ I've never been told that I can't play a certain character in a school play because of my race. I've never been told that I *have to* play a certain character in a school play because of my race.

- ❖ Nobody ever makes weird comments about my hair, my cultural foods, my cultural clothes, my accent, my parents' accents, or my cultural and religious holidays that make me uncomfortable.

- ❖ My cultural or religious holidays are celebrated by the entire country.

- ❖ I've never had to explain my cultural holidays or traditions to my classmates.

- ❖ My school teaches about many people from history who are the same race as me.

❖ My parents taught me that we "don't see color."

❖ My parents rarely, if ever, have conversations about our race with me.

❖ I've never felt or been told that I am less attractive because of my race.

❖ Most of the protagonists in the fiction books we read at school are the same race as me.

❖ Most of the protagonists in popular TV shows and movies are the same race as me.

❖ People of my race have never historically faced discrimination, enslavement, genocide, land theft, segregation, or other forms of oppression based on race.

❖ I don't feel very comfortable or confident having conversations about my race and racism, because they are not conversations I have often.

❖ I've never been mistaken for another person who is the same race as me.

The more statements that you were able to check off this list, the more likely it is that you hold white privilege.

White privilege is only something that white people (or people who look or pass as white) own. However, there are many other types of privileges that people may hold or not hold, including class privilege, gender privilege, sexuality privilege, age privilege, and able-bodied privilege. The word *privilege* doesn't mean that you live a rich and fancy life, where you've never had to struggle or have a negative experience. What it does mean, however, is that your negative experiences or struggles usually aren't because of the identity where you have privilege.

> What positive experiences do you think white privilege gives white people?

> What negative experiences do you think white privilege protects white people from?

As a Black person, I do not hold white privilege, and therefore I have had many negative experiences and struggles because of racism. However, as somebody who does not have a disability, I do hold able-bodied privilege and have never had a negative experience or struggle because of a disability.

I don't hold racial or white privilege, but I do hold able-bodied privilege. Both things are true at the same time, but they don't cancel each other out. Being Black doesn't mean that I don't have other privileges, just like being white doesn't mean a person doesn't experience other forms of discrimination. We have to be aware of the parts of our identities where we don't have privilege and the parts where we do.

> Having white privilege means that the color
> of your skin is like a passport or special ticket
> that allows you access to things like safety,
> opportunities, comfort, representation, and so
> much more that BIPOC don't generally have.

WHY DO WE NEED TO LOOK AT WHITE PRIVILEGE?

If you are white or have white privilege, you may be thinking, "But I didn't ask for this privilege! I didn't ask to be born white or for other people to not be born white. And I don't want white privilege. I don't think it's fair or right!"

If you are not white or don't have white privilege, you may be thinking, "But I didn't ask to be born the race that I am, and I don't think it's fair that I should be disadvantaged because of the color of my skin. It's not right!"

I completely understand, and I agree. Science has

proven that biologically, we are all one race, and no race is superior or inferior to another. Therefore, there is no reason why one race should have more advantages in society than any other. But we cannot begin to create a world like that until we understand the world that we currently have.

We cannot dismantle what we cannot see. We cannot challenge what we don't understand. We need to look at white privilege so that we can start making the *invisible knapsacks* visible and challenge society to stop giving some people advantages over others.

RECAP, REFLECT, RESPOND

RECAP

White privilege is a term that describes the unearned advantages, benefits, and immunities that white and white-passing people receive because of their race. Peggy McIntosh describes white privilege as "an invisible package of unearned assets that I can count on cashing in each day, but about which I was 'meant' to remain oblivious."

REFLECT

* How does talking about white privilege make you feel?

* Why do you think society is currently set up to give people who are white or who look white this privilege? Why do you think it denies people who are not white this privilege?

* Has a parent or adult ever talked to you about what it means to be your race? Have they ever talked to you about white privilege? What conversations do you now want to have with them about white privilege?

RESPOND

How People with White Privilege Can Respond to White Privilege:

❖ Have conversations with your family members, white friends, and white teachers about what it means to have white privilege. Make the *invisible knapsack* visible by pointing out all the ways you are advantaged over BIPOC.

❖ Start to play closer attention to how your BIPOC friends, schoolmates, and family members may be treated differently because of their race. If somebody white is treating them negatively because of the color of their skin, speak up and say something to defend them. Let them know you are on their side.

❖ Don't ask BIPOC rude questions or make unsolicited comments about their hair, cultural traditions, where they "really" come from, and so on. It's definitely okay to be curious and to ask polite questions about people who are different from you so you can learn more about them, but it's not okay to treat BIPOC as if they are not normal like you. Don't make BIPOC feel like they are different or other.

❖ Ask your teachers to provide more diverse lessons and books about people of other races. Ask your parents to ask your school to do so too. Let them know that you would like more positive representation of BIPOC historical figures, leaders, and book protagonists. (And not just about slavery, the civil rights movement, or experiencing racism. Although the heroes who have fought these battles are definitely important and should be studied, they should not be the only people or stories studied.)

How People Who Don't Have White Privilege Can Respond to White Privilege:

❖ Ask your teachers to provide more diverse lessons and books about people of other races. Ask your parents to ask your school to do so too. Let them know that you would like more positive representation of BIPOC historical figures, leaders, and book protagonists. (And not just about slavery, the civil rights movement, or experiencing racism. Although the heroes who have fought these battles are definitely important and should be studied, they should not be the only people or stories studied.)

❖ Know that you have the same right to belong and be represented as white people. Don't ever be ashamed of your race, your ethnicity, your cultural traditions, or your history. Stand tall and be proud of who you are. And if someone ever makes you feel different or other or tries to exclude you because of your race, speak clearly to them and let them know that you love every bit of who you are. Just because we currently live in a world that privileges white people doesn't mean that being white is inherently a privilege. Being who *you* are is the real privilege.

CHAPTER 6

white fragility

Most of the schools that I attended until I was fifteen years old were predominantly white and Christian. I was always the only Black student in my class and one of the very few Black students at the entire school. My younger brother and I were also always the only Muslim students in the whole school. My mother started to talk to me about race and being different from a really young age, because she knew that every day I went into school, I was seen as different and probably treated as different too. Because she started talking to me about race from such a young age, I've never felt uncomfortable talking about race and racism. It's something that I had to be aware of from early on and something that I had to learn how to navigate so that I could survive and thrive in my life.

On the other hand, I'm pretty sure that none of my white school friends had regular conversations about race, racism, and white privilege with their parents. Having white privilege meant being seen as the norm and not experiencing racism, so it was never a topic of conversation for them. While it may be a great privilege to never have to think about your race or racism, the problem is that they would grow up to become adults who felt really uncomfortable talking about race, racism, and what it means to be white. Many white people often feel this discomfort during conversations about race, and they often react defensively. This defensive reaction is called *white fragility*.

WHAT IS WHITE FRAGILITY?

White fragility is a term coined by American author Robin DiAngelo, who defines it as ***"a state in which even a minimum amount of racial stress becomes intolerable, triggering a range of defensive moves."***

WHAT DOES THIS MEAN? LET'S BREAK IT DOWN!

- *"A state"*: A way of feeling or being.
- *"in which even a minimum amount of racial stress"*: Where even the slightest conversation or interaction about race and racism.
- *"becomes intolerable"*: Becomes so unbearably uncomfortable.
- *"triggering a range of defensive moves"*: That it results in a person who has white privilege negatively reacting in ways to try to defend themselves.

The word *fragile* is used to describe the inability to hold even the slightest pressure when it comes to racial conversations or interactions. Because people who have white privilege are so unfamiliar with having conversations about white privilege or racism, their minds often perceive the interaction as dangerous, and they have a reaction of white fragility.

If you have white privilege, perhaps you felt a little of this when we went through the last chapter on white privilege. This is completely normal if you haven't been having regular conversations about race and what it means to have white privilege. It's completely new territory to you, and you may feel a range of different emotions, like confusion, guilt, shame, anger, and sadness. White fragility doesn't mean that you are weak, but it does mean that as a person who has white privilege, you haven't been given enough opportunities to practice the skill of confidently talking about race and racism.

There are two main reasons why white fragility happens: lack of exposure to conversations about racism and lack of understanding of what white supremacy actually is. Let's look at these reasons in a bit more depth.

1. LACK OF EXPOSURE TO CONVERSATIONS ABOUT RACISM

White privilege protects people who have it from having to discuss the causes and effects of racism. The privilege of whiteness means that one's day-to-day life isn't affected by skin color, so conversations about racism are usually very short and simple.

Conversations like the ones we're having in this book don't happen often, even between adults. And if you are white, you might not have had conversations about race and racism at all.

FOR PEOPLE WHO HAVE WHITE PRIVILEGE, THE CONVERSATIONS ABOUT RACE ARE USUALLY STATEMENTS LIKE THE FOLLOWING:

- ◆ "We don't see color."
- ◆ "There's only one race—the human race."
- ◆ "It doesn't matter if a person is white, black, red, yellow, blue, green, or purple. We are all the same."
- ◆ "It's rude to say someone is Black."
- ◆ "Racism is bad."

These statements may be very well-meaning, but they are not nuanced or multilayered enough to give a deep understanding of white supremacy and racism, and they don't equip people with white privilege with the tools to be able to talk about race without having a white fragility reaction. Not being exposed to regular and meaningful conversations about race leaves many young people with white privilege to grow up into adults who have a lot of white fragility.

On the other hand, if you are a BIPOC, your parents have probably had to talk to you about race and racism and how to survive and navigate various situations where people may treat you negatively because of the color of your skin. Perhaps you've had to have "the talk" about how to interact with police officers. Maybe a parent explained to you that the societal rules that apply to you don't apply to your white friends. Or maybe you've had a racist incident happen to you. For BIPOC, racism is not a conversation topic that we can avoid.

2. LACK OF UNDERSTANDING OF WHAT WHITE SUPREMACY ACTUALLY IS

The reason we started our journey with some brief history lessons beginning in the fifteenth century is because without a deep understanding of what white supremacy is, how it started, how it spread, and how it has harmed people around the world, it is almost impossible to have a real conversation about it or how to dismantle it. If your understanding of racism and white supremacy does not include historical and modern-day context, then you are going to struggle when it comes to conversations about race.

If you have white privilege, you may assume that what is being criticized is your white skin and how good of a person you are, rather than the fact that you benefit from a system of oppression that harms BIPOC (in ways that you aren't even aware of).

Similarly, while many BIPOC have conversations

about racism from a young age, those conversations aren't often about the history and breadth of white supremacy. Racism is not just about racial slurs, police brutality, and neo-Nazis, and it's not just confined to a single country.

The more we understand what white supremacy actually is, the more confident we all become to talk about it and fight it.

HOW DOES WHITE FRAGILITY SHOW UP?

A white fragility reaction is usually about the person with white privilege trying to protect themselves from being called racist. They don't want to feel like they've done something wrong. Being told they've been racist makes them feel like they are a bad person. The problem is, the defensive reaction itself ends up harming BIPOC. Reactions of anger, the silent treatment, denial, telling the authorities, and crying when you've done something that was (unintentionally) racist means that the person with white privilege is now seen as the victim—even though it was them that actually caused harm in the first place. White fragility is often quite violent in its

nature, because it paints BIPOC as mean, overly sensitive, or even as liars.

The impact of this is that the BIPOC is now hurt
twice: first when the person with white privilege was
racist to them, and again when they experience a white
fragility reaction.

WHEN PEOPLE WITH WHITE PRIVILEGE ARE CONFRONTED WITH A RACIST CONVERSATION OR INTERACTION, WHITE FRAGILITY CAN SHOW UP AS AN EMOTIONAL RESPONSE IN THE FOLLOWING WAYS:

* **ANGER:** They feel like they are being accused of
  something that they didn't do. They start arguing
  back to defend themselves, or they tell BIPOC that
  they are the ones being mean or racist to them.
  Maybe they decide that they're not going to talk to
  the other people involved anymore because of what
  they accused them of. Maybe they decide to tell an
  authority figure or institution about the ways they
  are being attacked.

* **SHAME:** They feel ashamed for being called out
  for saying something that was hurtful. They start
  crying because they feel so ashamed that others
  can't see the goodness of their heart. Or maybe they

feel like the other person is trying to make them feel ashamed for being white. They get angry again.

❖ **FEAR:** They don't know what they are supposed to do now, and they are scared of saying the wrong thing in case they accidentally say something racist again. They don't apologize or ask more questions. They simply go quiet and leave the conversation. On the other hand, they may be so afraid of being seen as a bad person that they keep talking to try and prove that they didn't do anything racist and that they are a good person.

❖ **IRRITATION:** They don't understand why race is being brought into the conversation. They become irritated and claim that the "race card" is being pulled or that BIPOC are being too sensitive. They may flip things around and paint themselves as the innocent victim who didn't do anything wrong and is being attacked for no reason.

❖ **SADNESS:** This often isn't sadness that they've caused racist harm but instead sadness that they feel they are being called out for no reason. They are sad because they feel like race has been brought into the conversation when it doesn't need to be. This is because they cannot see the ways in which white

supremacy and their white privilege are big parts of
the interaction.

❖ **ANXIETY:** They may feel anxious about talking about
race, racism, and what it means to be white. They
may also feel like talking about these topics is frustrating, unsafe, or hurtful to them. (Remember:
racism is frustrating, unsafe, and hurtful to BIPOC,
not to people who have white privilege.)

ASK YOURSELF

• If you have white privilege, have you ever experienced white fragility? If you are a BIPOC, has a
  person with white privilege ever had a reaction of
  white fragility toward you?
• What did this reaction look like?
• How did you feel at the time it was happening, and
  how do you feel about it now?

WHY DO WE NEED TO LOOK AT WHITE FRAGILITY?

Conversations about race and white supremacy are by
their very nature uncomfortable. While I may be comfortable talking about race, I still find it painful to talk about

racism because it has hurt and killed so many people. Racial conversations often come loaded with historical and present-day events and experiences that have caused pain, shame, and inequality. White fragility prevents people who have white privilege from having a conversation about racism without falling apart. If we cannot talk about racism, especially the ways in which some people benefit from it while other people are harmed, then we will never be able to change how things are.

White fragility not only gets in the way of antiracism, it also sustains white supremacy. If people with white privilege are more concerned about being *seen* as good, rather than actually *doing* good, they continue to uphold racism—which is the exact opposite of what they want to do!

White fragility therefore makes people with white privilege dangerous to BIPOC. And it shuts down communication between the two groups. Without communication, nothing changes.

So what's the answer to white fragility? *Racial resilience.*

People who have white privilege must become more resilient when it comes to having conversations about race, racism, and white supremacy.

> **WHAT IS RESILIENCE?**
> ◆ Resilience is the ability to recover or bounce back
>   from a tough situation. In this case, the tough situ-
>   ation is having conversations about racism.

Let's think about the difference between a mirror
and an elastic band.

If pressure is applied to a mirror, like when something hard is thrown at it, it cracks. It is not a resilient
material; it is fragile.

If pressure is applied to an elastic band, it is
stretched, but it usually doesn't break. It stretches,
and when you release it, it bounces back to its normal
shape. It may be a little looser than it was before you
stretched it, but it didn't break. In fact, it's designed to
be stretched so that it can be wrapped around things. It
is not a fragile material; it is resilient.

If you have white privilege and you consider yourself
to be like the mirror, when pressure is applied to you
through a conversation about racism, then most likely
you will crack and have a defensive reaction of white
fragility. But if you regard yourself as an elastic band,
you may be stretched by the conversation, but you can

still bounce back. The stretching still feels like anger, shame, confusion, and all those totally normal human feelings, but you don't stay like that. You bounce back. And what can you do when you bounce back? You can apologize. You can ask for further clarification about what you did. You can try to make amends. And you can know not to cause the same sort of harm next time.

Right now, we need more elastic band people than mirror people. We need people with white privilege who are resilient when it comes to conversations about racism. And the way to become resilient is to learn more about white supremacy and expose yourself to more conversations about racism.

RECAP, REFLECT, RESPOND

RECAP

White fragility is a term coined by Robin DiAngelo that is defined as "a state in which even a minimum amount of racial stress becomes intolerable, triggering a range of defensive moves." White fragility is the fight, flight, or freeze reaction that many people with white privilege often have when it comes to having conversations about racism.

REFLECT

❖ How do you think white fragility prevents people with white privilege from really being able to empathize with BIPOC who experience racism?

❖ How might people who have white privilege have deeper friendships with BIPOC if they can change from a mirror reaction of fragility to an elastic band reaction of resilience?

RESPOND

How People with White Privilege Can Respond to White Fragility:

❖ Learn more about the history and impact of white supremacy and racism. You can do this by reading books, watching videos, and listening to podcasts. I've included some recommended resources for you at the back of this book.

❖ Expose yourself to more conversations about race and racism—with people of all races. Talk to your friends, family, classmates, and teachers about these topics. Ask lots of questions to help you understand further. Talk about your feelings with someone who is also practicing antiracism. It's normal to feel shame, anger, and confusion as we practice antiracism. Talk it out with somebody who understands.

❖ Begin to see yourself as an elastic band instead of a mirror. When you notice yourself feeling those uncomfortable feelings, take a few deep breaths and try to recover. Remember, you are not being attacked for being white, and nobody is saying that being white is bad or that *you* are bad. Instead, racial conversations are about recognizing that you hold a privilege that BIPOC don't and that you and other white people may be causing harm in ways that you don't realize. Listen to what is being said, allow yourself to feel how you feel, and then bounce back.

How People Who Don't Have White Privilege Can Respond to White Fragility:

❖ Be aware that many people who do have white privilege will often have a reaction of white fragility when it comes to conversations about racism. This is true even for adults! Remember that having white privilege means that they don't often have the kinds of conversations about racism that you have had. However, and this is really important, understand that you do not have to accept a reaction of white fragility. You do not have to comfort, soothe, or apologize for respectfully saying something that causes a white fragility reaction. They are allowed to feel how they feel, but you do not have to take responsibility for their feelings. You are only responsible for your own feelings.

❖ If you have experienced harm because of racism, your first priority is to take care of yourself. Do not be afraid that if you say how you really feel about racism that people with white privilege will be hurt by your truth. The more you speak your truth, the more empowered we all become to fight white supremacy. Of course, it is important for us all to be kind and compassionate to one another. But know that part of antiracism practice is also not allowing white supremacy behaviors like white fragility to harm us.

❖ Here are some responses you can give to someone who has a white fragility reaction toward you:

  ❖ *I understand that this conversation is upsetting to you, but what you said to me was very hurtful and racist. You owe me an apology.*

  ❖ *I understand that this conversation is upsetting to you, but what you said to me was very hurtful and racist. I'm going to leave this conversation now to protect myself from any further harm.*

  ❖ *I know that you are upset by this conversation, but it is not my responsibility to take care of your feelings. I suggest talking this out with a white adult who is learning about antiracism who can help you sort through your feelings.*

  ❖ *Just because this conversation is upsetting to you doesn't mean that what you said or did wasn't harmful. I need you to take responsibility for your words and actions and apologize for the harm you caused me.*

  ❖ *Here is how I would like you to make amends for what you said or did...*

✧   *I refuse to continue this conversation if you are unwilling to really listen and understand why what you said or did was racist.*

✧   *As a BIPOC, my antiracism practice is about practicing self-love and self-honoring. If you are unwilling to move past your white fragility, then I can no longer be in this conversation or interaction with you.*

CHAPTER 7

tone policing

Serena Williams is arguably one of the greatest professional tennis players, if not athletes, of all time. Serena
and her older sister, Venus, have been playing tennis
since they were children, and both are former world
number one ranked players. At the time of writing this
book, Serena has also won twenty-three Grand Slam
single titles, which is the most by any player in the open
era (since 1968). She is an inspiring role model to young
people and adults around the world.

However, over the course of her trailblazing career,
she has experienced racist and sexist treatment both on
and off the court. Over the years, she has been compared

to a gorilla because of her physical shape and dark skin, experienced extra unnecessary drug tests, and had her outfits policed.

During her 2018 U.S. Open final match against tennis champion Naomi Osaka (a woman of mixed Haitian and Japanese descent), Williams was called on for a number of violations that confused both her and the crowd. One of these charges was for "verbal abuse" after she called the umpire a "thief."

In a *Newsweek* article, Dr. Crystal Fleming, a professor of sociology and Africana studies at Stony Brook University, wrote, "Watching the greatest player of all time get tone-policed by a petty man abusing his power was both heartbreaking and infuriating—especially as a black woman... Male players, like James Blake and John McEnroe, have come forward to affirm that they have said much worse to chair umpires without being penalized or fined."

Many male players have said far worse things to umpires in their matches than Williams said to the umpire at the 2018 Open. However, Williams argued that she was treated differently because she was a woman. And though she didn't say it, many Black women, including myself and Crystal Fleming, felt it was specifically because she was a Black woman, because Black women are often *tone policed* when expressing strong emotions.

WHAT IS TONE POLICING?

Tone policing is a tactic used by those who have privilege to silence those who do not have privilege. This is done by focusing on the *tone* of what is being said rather than the actual *content*. A person with white privilege who is tone policing cares more about *how* BIPOC say something and not *what* they're saying. Essentially, BIPOC are expected to talk and communicate in ways that people with white privilege decide are correct. And when it comes to conversations about racism, it often looks like asking BIPOC to communicate in ways that don't trigger white fragility.

Tone policing, or the possibility of it, is a constant drain on the psyches of BIPOC. At school, kids of color are sometimes tone policed by white teachers for not speaking English in ways that white people do. Other times, the opposite happens, where white people are surprised that kids of color speak the same way they do, often calling them "eloquent," even though they don't call other white people that for speaking the same way.

In an attempt to avoid the possibility of being tone policed, many BIPOC will often subconsciously police their own tone in order to avoid having to deal with white fragility. As a Black writer, it often feels like I'm being pulled in several different directions when trying to express myself. Am I coming across as too angry? Am I coming across as too soft?

It is often a big shock when BIPOC decide that they will no longer police their own tone and instead will fully be themselves and express their full range of feelings about racism. People with white privilege wonder with confusion and frustration, *Where is this anger coming from?* What they do not realize is that giving ourselves the freedom to express our true emotions is actually an important part of practicing antiracism.

HOW DOES TONE POLICING SHOW UP?

Tone policing can look like criticizing or telling BIPOC

off for using tones that are "too angry," or refusing to listen to or believe BIPOC until they change their tone. Other times, it may look like someone with white privilege celebrating BIPOC when they use tones considered more soft, eloquent, and soothing.

TONE POLICING HAPPENS WHEN PEOPLE WITH WHITE PRIVILEGE SAY OR THINK THE FOLLOWING THINGS TO BIPOC DURING RACIAL CONVERSATIONS:

* *I wish that you would say what you're saying in a nicer way.*
* *I can't take in what you're telling me about your lived experiences because you sound too angry.*
* *Your tone is too aggressive.*
* *The way you are talking about racism is making me feel ashamed.*
* *The way you are talking about racism is hateful or divisive.*
* *You should talk to white people in a more civil way if you want us to join your cause.*
* *The way you are talking about this issue is not helpful.*
* *If you would just calm down, then maybe I will want to listen to you.*

❖ *You are bringing too much negativity. You should focus on the positive instead.*

Tone policing does not only have to be spoken out loud. People with white privilege often police the tone of BIPOC in their thoughts or behind closed doors, because they know that doing so out loud may be considered racist. But just because someone doesn't say it out loud doesn't mean it doesn't cause harm. Tone policing can also be expressed in a disapproving look, refusal to listen to BIPOC, and not believing BIPOC when they share about their experiences of racism because of the tone that they are using.

An example of explicit or direct tone policing is when a person with white privilege says, "Maybe more white people would want to talk about racism if Black people weren't so angry all the time."

An example of implicit or indirect tone policing is when a person with white privilege thinks in their mind about BIPOC, *That Black person must be less smart than me because they talk so ghetto.*

**TONE POLICING DOESN'T JUST HAPPEN
DURING CONVERSATIONS ABOUT RACE. IT
CAN ALSO LOOK LIKE THE FOLLOWING:**

- ❖ Judging BIPOC for being too loud
- ❖ Calling Black people ghetto
- ❖ Judging Black people for using African American Vernacular English (AAVE) instead of Standard English
- ❖ Judging BIPOC as not "talking properly" when they don't talk like white people

ASK YOURSELF
- ◆ If you have white privilege, have you ever tone policed a BIPOC?
- ◆ If you are a BIPOC, have you ever been tone policed?
- ◆ Was the tone policing explicit or implicit?
- ◆ How did it make you feel then, and how do you feel about it now?

WHY DO WE NEED TO LOOK AT TONE POLICING?

Tone policing is about control and power exercised by people with white privilege over BIPOC. It reinforces white supremacist norms of how BIPOC are "supposed" to show up in order to be considered fully human by people with white privilege. It is a way of keeping BIPOC in line and disempowered. When people with white privilege insist that they will not believe or give credibility or attention to BIPOC until they speak in a tone that suits them, they are upholding the racist idea that white people's standards and ways of being are superior. When people with white privilege try to control the tone of how BIPOC are supposed to talk about racism, they are reinforcing the white supremacist ideology that white people know best and are the best.

Before colonialism, BIPOC existed and spoke in ways that were the standard for them and in their own languages. When European nations colonized Black and Brown countries, they insisted that Black and Brown people speak English and do so in the way and manner that white people do. When BIPOC speak in their own languages or speak English in the way that feels right for them (especially when it comes to speaking about racism), this is often perceived as a threat to white domination over BIPOC. Tone policing is a subtle, often unconscious, everyday way that white people try to continue enforcing that white domination.

It is "communication colonization," and it is something that we must all free ourselves from.

Lastly, tone policing is a form of psychological manipulation that seeks to sow seeds of doubt in people by making them question their memory, perception, and sanity. Serena Williams experienced this during and after the 2018 Open. Many people tried to say that she was too sensitive, or that she was jealous of her opponent, Naomi Osaka (who went on to win the match), or that she was playing the "gender card." But after the match, Williams congratulated Osaka for the win and told her she was proud of her. Her angry reaction wasn't about her opponent; it was about the tone policing she had experienced during the match that she believed her male opponents did not experience.

BIPOC's rage is often seen as unacceptable and dangerous, and we are often tone policed for it as a way to keep us in check. This is dehumanizing, because to be human is to feel. And BIPOC have a lot of feelings about the pain and violence of racism, going back generations. We are entitled to express our personal and collective pain about racism in ways that feel human to us. In the past, I have been criticized by white people when I talk about racism in ways that make them feel uncomfortable. They ask me to say what I am saying but to take my emotions out of what I'm saying. Essentially, to be neutral, like a robot. I refuse to do that, because part of my antiracism work as a Black woman is to act and live like a whole human being who has the right to express herself authentically—even if it triggers a reaction of white fragility.

When we understand how tone policing works and why it happens, we can change our behaviors to allow BIPOC the full expression of their humanity.

RECAP, REFLECT, RESPOND

RECAP

Tone policing is a tactic used by those who have (white) privilege to silence those who do not, by focusing on the tone of what is being said rather than the actual content. Tone policing does not only have to be spoken out loud publicly. People with white privilege often tone police BIPOC in their thoughts or behind closed doors.

REFLECT

❖   How is tone policing an example of white supremacy? *(Reminder: white supremacy says white people deserve to be dominant over nonwhite people.)*

❖   What emotional and mental damage do you think tone policing does to BIPOC?

RESPOND

How People with White Privilege Can Respond to Tone Policing:

❖   Tone policing is usually preceded by white fragility. Because of what we covered in our last chapter, a white fragility reaction should now be easier to spot. If you feel yourself having a white fragility reaction because of a racial conversation, take a moment to breathe and check in with yourself before asking BIPOC to change their tone. Usually what's happening is that you want BIPOC to change their tone so that you can get rid of your uncomfortable feelings. But BIPOC should not have to change their tone to express their pain about racism. Allow BIPOC to authentically express themselves, and don't try to shut their emotions down by tone policing them. Remember that BIPOC authentically expressing themselves is not a threat to you.

❖ Pay more attention to your thoughts. When you find yourself implicitly tone policing BIPOC, catch your thoughts and change them. For example, if you find yourself thinking, *Black people are so angry when they're talking about racism*, change it to *Black people have the right to be angry when talking about racism because racism hurts and kills Black people.*

❖ Understand that there are many ways to talk in the English language. AAVE and other forms of English are just as acceptable as Standard English. Part of practicing antiracism is changing our mindset to stop seeing white ways of being as the only correct

ways of being. Other ways of speaking and expressing ourselves are just as standard and normal as
white ways of speaking and expressing ourselves.

How People Who Don't Have White Privilege Can
Respond to Tone Policing:

❖ Do not ever feel you have to change your tone to
express your feelings about racism. Authentically
express yourself, and don't allow people with white
privilege to make you feel your feelings or self-
expression are not valid.

❖ Don't try to tone police yourself. Sometimes BIPOC
(myself included!) tone police ourselves in our own
minds as a way to protect ourselves from other
people doing it to us. You are entitled to your own
voice and your own way of communicating.

❖ If somebody tries to tone police you, clearly let them
know that you are entitled to talk in ways that feel
authentic to you.

❖ Understand that there are many ways to talk in the
English language. AAVE and other forms of English
are just as acceptable as Standard English. Part of
practicing antiracism is changing our mindset to
stop seeing white ways of being as the only correct

way of being. Other ways of speaking and expressing ourselves are just as standard and normal as
white ways of speaking and expressing ourselves.

CHAPTER 8

white silence

Martin Luther King Jr. Malala Yousafzai. Rosa Parks. Nelson Mandela. Harriet Tubman. Gloria Steinem. What do these people have in common?

They are some of the most recognized role models and activists in history. They are people of different genders, generations, and races, but the one thing that binds them together is the courage they have had to use their voices to call out injustice so that we can build a fairer world. These are people who have refused to stay silent.

While many see them as some of the inspiring change makers of their time, others have called them troublemakers, lawbreakers, and extremists. The work they have done in the world has helped us to fight racism and sexism, but they have all paid a price for it: physical attacks, ostracism, imprisonment, and even death. Despite understanding the risks involved in using their voices, they have chosen to do so anyway because of their strong beliefs that silence means agreement with injustice. They would rather use their voices for good and be criticized by those who were maintaining the status quo than stay silent and be a part of injustice by not calling it out. As a result of their commitment to speaking truth to power, millions of people have been inspired by them to also use their voices to advocate for change.

It takes courage to speak out against injustice. But if people don't speak out, things stay the same. And when it comes to white supremacy, things have stayed largely the same because of *white silence*.

WHAT IS WHITE SILENCE?

White silence is exactly what it sounds like. It's when people with white privilege stay silent when it comes to issues of racism and white supremacy. Their silence sends a message that they do not disagree with the injustice of racism. They uphold white supremacy because they don't speak out against it.

In our last chapter, we covered tone policing, which is how people with white privilege silence BIPOC. Today we are unpacking white silence, which is about how people with white privilege stay silent about racism.

People with white privilege often engage in white silence because they are scared of what might happen to them if they speak up. The leaders, organizers, and participants of antiracist civil rights movements have often been BIPOC who have felt that silence is not an option. They knew that, as the Black writer Audre Lorde said, "their silence would not protect them" from experiencing racism. However, for people with white privilege, silence *is* a form of protection. It's a way to avoid being criticized, hurt, rejected, and punished. For people who experience racism, those things can happen whether we are silent or not.

In his "Letter from a Birmingham Jail," Martin Luther King Jr. wrote, "We will have to repent in this generation not merely for the hateful words and actions of the bad people but for the appalling silence of the good people."

What Dr. King meant by this was that white supremacy is not just upheld by the people who are actively racist. It is also maintained by the people who say nothing. Saying nothing is saying something. It's saying "I agree with the way things are." That's why Dr. King called this silence *appalling*.

The burden of speaking out against racism shouldn't only fall on the shoulders of BIPOC. In fact, it's the responsibility of all people who have white privilege to speak out against racism.

HOW DOES WHITE SILENCE SHOW UP?

Here are a few examples of white silence in action.

- ❖ People with white privilege staying silent (or making excuses/changing the subject/leaving the room) when family members or friends with white privilege make racist jokes or comments.
- ❖ People with white privilege staying silent when their classmates or friends of color are discriminated against.
- ❖ People with white privilege staying silent when other white people treat their biracial or multiracial family members in racist ways.
- ❖ People with white privilege choosing not to engage in any conversations about race because of their white fragility.
- ❖ People with white privilege choosing not to attend protest marches against racism like Black Lives Matter or protests for immigrants at risk.

❖   People with white privilege staying silent when their favorite white celebrity is called out for racist behavior or defending that celebrity's racism.

❖   People with white privilege staying silent when they witness other people using their white privilege, white fragility, or tone policing against BIPOC.

❖   People with white privilege not sharing social media posts about race and racism because of the way it might affect how other white people see them. Staying silent about antiracism for fear of losing friends and followers.

ASK YOURSELF

◆   If you have white privilege, have you ever been in a situation where you were silent about racism that you were seeing?

◆   If you are a BIPOC, have you ever been in a situation with a person with white privilege who stayed silent when racism was happening to you or another BIPOC?

◆   How did you feel about it then, and how do you feel about it now?

JULIETTE HAMPTON MORGAN

Juliette Hampton Morgan was a white woman who found white silence appalling. Morgan lived in Montgomery, Alabama, during segregation and came from a wealthy and prominent family. She worked as a librarian. However, because she suffered from anxiety attacks, she was unable to drive herself to and from work. Instead, she took the Montgomery city buses, which were segregated, and that is where she witnessed Black people being humiliated and discriminated against by the white bus drivers.

Back then, it was the custom that Black passengers paid their bus fare at the front of the bus and then got off the bus and reentered through the back door. They were not allowed to use the front door with white people and had to sit at the back of the bus. One day, Morgan witnessed a Black woman pay her fare and exit the bus to reenter through the back door, but before she could do so, the white bus driver pulled away and drove off without her. Angry at what had just happened, Morgan jumped up and pulled the emergency cord, demanding the Black woman be let on the bus. After that incident, Morgan pulled the emergency cord every time she witnessed an incident of racist injustice.

Morgan not only used her voice on the city buses. She also wrote letters to the *Montgomery Advertiser*, the city's local newspaper, criticizing the injustices and demanding that the city's citizens do something about it. This was in 1939, sixteen years before the Montgomery bus boycott sparked by the arrest of Rosa Parks. When Morgan spoke out and wrote these letters, she was alone. As a white woman of economic privilege, she was expected to stay quiet and go along with how things were. Other white people, including her own mother and friends, were so angered by her using her voice that she was mocked, attacked, and threatened. If Morgan were alive today, she would have written online articles, published social media posts, and posted YouTube videos to protest racism. She would have used her voice in whatever medium was popular to speak out against racism.

WHY DO WE NEED TO LOOK AT WHITE SILENCE?

On the surface of it, white silence seems benign or non-threatening. And if not benign, then it could at least be believed to be neutral, like the old saying, "If you can't say anything nice, then don't say anything at all." But white silence is not neutral. Instead, it's a method of protecting one's white privilege and therefore also about protecting white supremacy. It protects people with white privilege from having to deal with the harm of white supremacy. And it protects white supremacy from being challenged, which means it stays firmly in place.

Here is a radical idea that I would like you to understand: white silence is violence. It actively protects the system. It says *I am okay with the way things are because they do not negatively affect me and because I enjoy the benefits I receive with white privilege.* When I talk about white silence being violent, I am not talking about people with white privilege not saying anything when they see someone making a racist comment or perpetrating a racist hate crime. Those are extreme examples we don't necessarily see in our everyday lives. Remember, white supremacy is not just about individual acts of racism. Rather, it is a system of

oppression that seeps into and often forms the foundation of many of the normal spaces where we spend our
time—at home, on the street, at school, in after-school
clubs, in faith communities, on social media, and so
on. These spaces are often protected from obvious and
interpersonal acts of racism while allowing less obvious and institutional and structural racism to be part
of the accepted culture through white silence.

HERE ARE SOME EXAMPLES OF HOW PEOPLE WITH WHITE PRIVILEGE USE WHITE SILENCE IN THESE SPACES:

❖   At home, a grandfather who has white privilege
    makes a racist remark about People of Color. The
    grandson, who also has white privilege, hears the
    remark but doesn't say anything. He knows what
    his grandfather said was racist, but he stays silent
    because he doesn't want to challenge or upset him.

❖   On the street, a person with white privilege sees a
    white woman harassing a group of young People
    of Color who are hanging out. The white woman
    is threatening to call the police. The person with
    white privilege who is watching the scene play
    out walks past and says nothing. They stay silent
    because they don't want to get involved, and they

suspect the group of young People of Color have done something to warrant the harassment.

❖ At school, the reading books that are assigned by the teachers each year almost always feature white people, and when there are books about BIPOC, they are always about topics like slavery and racism. The students with white privilege stay silent about this and do not ask the teachers to assign more diverse books. They stay silent because for the most part, they hadn't even realized that the books weren't diverse.

❖ At an after-school drama club, the drama teacher only lets the BIPOC members play roles that are BIPOC characters. Often, the main characters are white, so the white members end up getting these roles. The white members do not ask the drama teacher to assign more "white" roles to BIPOC members. They stay silent because they also think that BIPOC members should also only play BIPOC roles.

❖ On social media, a young Black person publishes a TikTok video about the Black Lives Matter movement. A group of young white people from the same school begin to comment that Black people always make everything about race. Another student from the same school who has white privilege reads the comments. They don't agree with the other white students, but they don't say anything. They stay silent because they don't want to risk the other white students attacking them too. They don't want to lose friends or become unpopular, so they say nothing.

Think about all the places where you spend your time. Imagine if each time direct or indirect racism happened there, people with white privilege used their voices to challenge the culture and demand change instead of staying in white silence. Everyone's voices are needed to call out injustice, especially the voices of people who have white privilege. The voice of a person who has white privilege can become a weapon that is used to dismantle white supremacy.

At the same time, while speaking up, remember to *stay safe*. While it is absolutely crucial for us, especially those with white privilege, to speak out against racism, it's equally important to do so in a way that doesn't put us in the way of physical harm. If it's an unsafe situation, find a trusted adult, and let them know about the racism that's happening.

A QUICK NOTE FOR THE INTROVERTS
WHO HAVE WHITE PRIVILEGE:

Introversion is not an excuse to stay in white silence. As someone who is an introvert, I understand that our natural tendency and preference is to keep to ourselves and let the extroverts take center stage. However, when it comes to antiracism, using introversion as a reason to stay in silence is actually just an excuse to stay in your comfort zone.

You can be an introvert and protest racist actions like Rosa Parks. You can be an introvert and use writing to disrupt white supremacy like Juliette Hampton Morgan. You can be an introvert and lead a powerful movement like Nelson Mandela. You do not have to be the loudest voice. But you do need to use your voice. And every time you use your voice, you take us one step closer toward justice and freedom. Find the best way to use *your* voice.

ANNE BRADEN

Ann Braden was a white woman who chose to use her voice instead of staying silent. Born in Louisville, Kentucky, in 1924, Anne Braden was a civil rights activist, journalist, and educator who, with her white husband, Carl Braden, spoke out against racism and fought for racial justice. Anne Braden understood that staying silent was not an option, because she saw her silence as a loud message that she sided with white supremacy. As a southern white woman of her time, she was expected to uphold white supremacy, support segregation, and demean Black people. She chose to do the opposite. She said, "Either you find a way to oppose the evil, or the evil becomes part of you and you are a part of it, and it winds itself around your soul like the arms of an octopus... If I did not oppose it, I was...responsible for its sins."

Braden understood that her silence was not neutral—it was complicity. And she so strongly believed in the equality of people of all races that her conscience could not allow her to stay silent in the face of injustice. Our world desperately needs more people with white privilege like Braden who are willing to use their voices as weapons against white supremacy.

RECAP, REFLECT, RESPOND

RECAP

White silence is when people who have white privilege stay complicitly silent when it comes to issues of race and racism.

REFLECT

❖ Why do you think a lot of people with white privilege use white silence? What do you think they'll lose by speaking up, and what do you think they'll gain?

❖ How does staying silent about racism make people with white privilege complicit in racism?

❖ Who in your life and community may be hurting because of white silence?

❖ How do you think the world would be different if more people with white privilege stopped being silent and spoke out against racism?

RESPOND

How People with White Privilege Can Respond to White Silence:

❖ Research five white people from history and today who do not engage in white silence. Some historical examples from this chapter include Juliette Hampton Morgan and Anne Braden. Use these people as role models for how to speak out, and use your voice as a weapon against white supremacy.

❖ Think about some ways that you can start using your voice against racism by focusing on your strengths and the areas of your life that you are passionate about. Juliette Hampton Morgan used writing to express her message. American activist and former football quarterback Colin Kaepernick used kneeling during the national anthem as a way to communicate his message. Patrisse Cullors, Dr. Opal Tometi, and Alicia Garza, the founders of Black Lives Matter, used a hashtag to begin their message. Find the method and medium that most excites you, and start speaking up.

How People Who Don't Have White Privilege Can Respond to White Silence:

❖ It has often fallen upon BIPOC to use their voices to speak out against racial injustice. If this is something that you want to do, do so proudly, knowing that you have every right to demand justice and a better world. Know that you stand on the shoulders of ancestors who have come before you who have used their voices to protest white supremacy.

❖   If there are people with white privilege in your life who care about you and are engaging in white silence, let them know that you need them to use their voices. Let them know that their white silence hurts you and people who look like you. Ask them to come out of their comfort zones of white privilege and use their voices to fight racism.

CHAPTER 9

white superiority

In 2008, American author Suzanne Collins published *The Hunger Games*, her first book in the dystopian trilogy. The book tells the story of sixteen-year-old protagonist Katniss Everdeen, who lives in the future in the postapocalyptic nation Panem. Katniss volunteers herself as a tribute for the annual televised battle royale to the death, the Hunger Games, in place of her younger sister, Primrose. The book was an instant success and gained worldwide fame. In 2012, the book came to theater screens and was released as a movie.

And that's when the trouble began.

The Hunger Games includes a character called

Rue, a twelve-year-old tribute from District 11 and the youngest tribute in the games. Rue helps and befriends Katniss during the games but is later tragically killed by one of the other tributes. Though Rue is only in the story for a short part of the games, she becomes a key part of Katniss's personal story and motivation as she later becomes the mockingjay. In the book, Collins describes Rue as having "dark brown skin and eyes" and "thick dark hair, dark satiny brown skin and golden eyes." However, many readers made the assumption that Rue was white. So when the movie trailer for *The Hunger Games* was released with the biracial actor Amandla Stenberg playing Rue, a tirade of racist comments were tweeted by *Hunger Games* readers. Here is a sampling of some of those tweets:

"why does Rue have to be black not gonna lie kinda ruined the movie"

"Awkward moment when Rue is some black girl and not the little blonde innocent girl you picture"

"EWW rue is black?? I'm not watching"

"some ugly little girl with nappy a** hair. Pissed me off. She was supposed to be cute and at least remind her of Prim!"

"Kk call me racist but when I found out rue was black her death wasn't as sad #ihatemyself"

"Why is Rue a little black girl? #sticktothebookdude"

"I was pumped about the Hunger Games. Until I learned that a black girl was playing Rue."

"And for the record, I'm still pissed that rue is black. Like you think she might have mentioned that...? Is that just me, or...."

> *"HOW IN THE WORLD ARE THEY GOING TO MAKE RUE A FREAKING BLACK B**** IN THE MOVIE?!?!?!??! Lolol not to be racist buuuuut...I'm angry now ;o"*

> *"Sense when has Rue been a n*****?"*

Despite Collins describing the character as having dark skin and later confirming in a media interview that Rue was African American, many readers felt offended, upset, and angry that Rue had been cast as Black in the movie. Their white imaginations had imagined her as white because her character in the story is innocent and because it is often white people who are cast as protagonists in books and movies. Unknowingly, they had bought into the racist idea that Black people should not be cast as characters that they resonate with—because Black people are not likable in the same way that white people are. This is *white superiority*.

WHAT IS WHITE SUPERIORITY?

Merriam-Webster defines *superior* as an adjective meaning "situated higher up; of higher rank, quality, or importance."

White superiority comes directly from white supremacy's belief that people with white or white-appearing skin are better than and therefore deserve to dominate over people with brown or black skin. Most people with white privilege are not consciously thinking that they are superior to BIPOC. Most are not harboring violently racist beliefs of superiority like those of the Ku Klux Klan and neo-Nazis. But white superiority can show up in more everyday ways, like getting upset that a character in a movie has been cast as Black.

THE IDEA OF WHITE SUPERIORITY IS LEARNED AT A VERY YOUNG AGE, AND THIS WAS DISCOVERED IN THE DOLL TESTS.

In the 1940s, husband and wife team and African American psychologists Dr. Kenneth Clark and Dr. Mamie Clark studied the psychological effects of racial segregation on African American children between the ages of three and seven. They showed the children identical dolls, with the only differences between them being skin color: half the dolls were white, and half were black. The children were asked to identify the races of the dolls and which color doll they preferred. Most of the children said they preferred the white doll, and they said more positive things about it than the black doll. The conclusion of the experiment was that prejudice, discrimination, and segregation had created a feeling of inferiority among African American children and damaged their self-esteem. In other words, many African American children were seeing white dolls and white people as superior, and black dolls and Black people as inferior.

In 2010, Dr. Margaret Beale Spencer, a

renowned child psychologist and university professor, was hired to re-create the doll tests for the modern age. This time, however, white children were tested as well as Black children, and images of white, Brown, and Black children were shown to the children. The tests showed that white children tended to describe images of white children with more positive attributes (like smart, good, and trustworthy) and images of children with darker skin with more negative attributes (like dumb, mean, bad, and ugly). The researchers called this phenomenon "white bias." The tests also showed that the Black children were far less likely to respond with white bias. At the end of the tests, Dr. Spencer concluded that while all children learn about racial stereotypes, white children tend to learn and believe those stereotypes more strongly than African American children.

The idea of whiteness being of higher rank, quality, or importance begins before we are even consciously aware of it. And if you have white privilege and are unaware of what it means to be white, this idea of superiority often goes largely unchallenged and becomes an internal unconscious truth. It is no surprise that around the world today, even in the Middle East where I live, it is far easier to find white dolls than black or brown dolls in toy shops. White dolls, like white people, are seen as more desirable and as the norm—superior in all ways to black and brown dolls and Black and Brown people.

HOW DOES WHITE SUPERIORITY SHOW UP?

Here are a few examples of white superiority in action. As you go through the list, think about whether you've ever thought or done these things.

❖ People with white privilege tone policing BIPOC (as discussed in chapter 7)

❖ Preferring and desiring European standards of beauty (like lighter or whiter skin tones, straighter hair). The doll tests illustrated this in horrifying ways, but so does the modern-day lack of representation of dark-skinned and kinky-haired women in movies, TV, magazines, and media.

❖ Believing African American Vernacular English (AAVE) is "ghetto" and thinking the correct way to talk is the way white people talk

❖ Primarily reading books by white authors

❖ Mainly supporting white leaders

❖ Primarily staying on the "white" side of town

❖ Believing that white people are generally smarter, cleaner, nicer, more attractive, more trustworthy, and kinder than BIPOC (whether consciously or unconsciously)

ASK YOURSELF
- ◆ What subtle messages do you receive from home, school, TV shows, movies, the internet and social media, or shops and businesses that people with white privilege are superior and BIPOC are inferior?
- ◆ What do those messages look and sound like?

WHY DO WE NEED TO LOOK AT WHITE SUPERIORITY?

The idea of white superiority is the very foundation of white supremacy. We continue to perpetuate white supremacy if we keep believing and acting like people with white privilege are superior to BIPOC. Again, it's important to remember that this belief is not necessarily a conscious one. It is often a deeply hidden, unconscious aspect of white supremacy that is hardly ever spoken about but practiced in daily life without even thinking about it.

The reality is, from as early as preschool, you are being conditioned to believe in white superiority and BIPOC inferiority. You are being taught white superiority through the way history is taught, the way race is talked about (or not talked about), the way white students and students of color are often treated differently, the lack of representation of BIPOC teachers, celebrities, and leaders, the way Black people are talked about at home and in the news, and through cultural appropriation and white saviorism (which we'll cover in chapters 15 and 17).

We need to look at white superiority so that we can begin to unravel it within ourselves and dismantle it within the spaces around us.

RECAP, REFLECT, RESPOND

RECAP

White superiority is the untrue and racist idea that people with white or white-passing skin are superior to and therefore deserve to dominate over people with black or brown skin.

REFLECT

* ❖ How do you think messages of racial superiority and inferiority cause harm as people grow up?
* ❖ If the ideas of white superiority and white bias start from a young age, what do you think needs to happen to change that? How can we get rid of this idea? What should children be taught instead?
* ❖ How do you think the world would be different if white superiority no longer existed?

RESPOND

White superiority is something that we are all conditioned into, because society is constantly reinforcing this idea that white people are smarter, wiser, more attractive, more innocent, and better. We must all constantly challenge the ways we have may bought into white superiority and BIPOC inferiority.

WHEN YOU NOTICE A THOUGHT OF WHITE SUPERIORITY OR BIPOC INFERIORITY ARISING WITHIN YOUR OWN MIND, STOP AND ASK YOURSELF FOUR QUESTIONS:

1. Why do I think that?
2. Where did I learn this thought?
3. How does this thought harm me?
4. How can I replace this thought with a thought that doesn't reinforce white superiority?

Every time you hear a person who has white privilege say something that sounds like white superiority, draw their attention to it. Let them know that their words are hurtful, even if they didn't mean it in a hurtful way. Invite them to learn about their own white bias.

CHAPTER 10

white exceptionalism

Dr. Ellen Pence was an American scholar and social activist who was born in 1948 in Minneapolis, Minnesota. As a young white girl, she grew up with a father who was blatantly racist and who preached about the natural "superiority" of white people. Despite her father's strong beliefs, she did not share his ideology. Instead, she sent her babysitting money to Martin Luther King Jr., attended marches, and went to confession to the Black priest at their mainly white parish. She believed that these things made her "one of the good ones," a white person who was not racist like her father.

However, as she grew up and became more involved in activism, she began to realize that maybe she wasn't as exceptional as she thought. She would often hear women of color accusing white women of racism, but she didn't understand why. As she later wrote, when she heard these critiques, she would think to herself, "Certainly, they didn't mean me—I had marched in Milwaukee. I too was oppressed by the white male. So when I heard women of color speaking of white privileges, I mentally inserted the word 'male': 'male white privileges.'"

It was only when a Black friend of hers named Ella Gross explained to her that she didn't want to recognize her own racism that Pence began to understand. She began to see that white women, who were oppressed by sexism by white men, did the same thing to women of color by oppressing them with racism.

She had thought that because she didn't hold outright racist beliefs like her father, she was not racist. But the deeper she examined herself and the activist movements she was involved in, the more she saw that she did indeed have racist thoughts, beliefs, and behaviors. She realized she was not an *exceptional white person* when it came to practicing racism.

WHAT IS WHITE EXCEPTIONALISM?

According to the *Cambridge Dictionary*, to be exceptional means to be "someone or something that is not included in a rule, group, or list or that does not behave in the expected way."

White exceptionalism is the belief that many people with white privilege often have about themselves that they are not racist, do not have racist thoughts, beliefs, or behaviors, and that they are "one of the good ones." That other white people are racist but they aren't. And that they are excluded from the effects, benefits, and conditioning of white supremacy, so they do not have to do antiracism work.

While it's true that some people proudly choose to be racists and white supremacists—like Ellen Pence's father—this does not exclude all other people with white privilege from benefiting from white supremacy and being racist to BIPOC, even though it may not be their intention.

The reason many people with white privilege fall into white exceptionalism is because they believe in what is called the "good/bad binary" of racism.

THAT BINARY LOOKS LIKE THIS:

❖ There are two types of people—good people and bad people.

❖ Racist people are bad people.

❖ Not racist people are good people.

❖ I am a good person. Therefore, I am not racist and could never be racist.

This binary may seem like it makes sense. Racism is indeed bad, and to do something racist is definitely a bad thing. However, racism isn't just when someone intentionally does something to harm BIPOC.

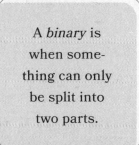

A *binary* is when something can only be split into two parts.

Racism is also when *good people* receive *white privilege* while BIPOC don't.

It's when *well-meaning people* react defensively with *white fragility* to BIPOC.

It's when *kind people* stay *silent* in the face of racism.

It's when *nice people* unknowingly believe they are *superior* to BIPOC.

Racism actually has nothing to do with whether a person with white privilege is a good person or a bad person. Instead, it's about who benefits from a world of white supremacy and who is harmed by it.

When a person with white privilege believes they are exceptional when it comes to racism, they believe that they do not benefit from white supremacy and that they do not subconsciously have racist thoughts, beliefs, and behaviors that harm BIPOC. Hopefully as you continue to read this book, you are beginning to see that this is just not possible and that it is the responsibility of *all* people with white privilege to practice antiracism.

HOW DOES WHITE EXCEPTIONALISM SHOW UP?

White exceptionalism shows up when people with white privilege believe the following:

❖ Racism is something that only some people with white privilege do.

❖ Being racially color blind (something we cover in chapter 12) means they can't be racist.

❖ Having BIPOC friends or family members means they can't be racist.

❖ Liking BIPOC celebrities, authors, YouTubers,

TikTokers, musicians, and social media influencers means they can't be racist.

❖ Being a nice, good, or kind person means they can't be racist.

❖ It's only racism when it's obviously harmful like name-calling or bullying but not when it's less obvious things like white silence and white superiority.

ASK YOURSELF

◆ If you have white privilege, how have you practiced white exceptionalism?

◆ If you are a BIPOC, how have people with white privilege in your life practiced white exceptionalism?

WHY DO WE NEED TO LOOK AT WHITE EXCEPTIONALISM?

In his 1963 "Letter from a Birmingham Jail," Martin Luther King Jr. identified white exceptionalism as one of the greatest barriers to Black people in their striving for freedom. White exceptionalism is not something that is practiced by outright proud white supremacists but rather by people who would consider themselves progressive, "nice" people who believe that racism is wrong. Martin Luther King Jr. called these people the "white moderates." He saw them as an even greater barrier to racial justice than those who were proud racists.

Below is his most famous passage from this essay:

> *First, I must confess that over the past few years I have been gravely disappointed with the white moderate. I have almost reached the regrettable conclusion that the Negro's great stumbling block in his stride toward freedom is not the White Citizen's Council-er or the Ku Klux Klanner, but the white moderate, who is more devoted to "order" than to justice; who prefers a negative peace which is the absence of tension to a positive peace which is the presence of justice; who constantly says: "I agree with you in the goal you seek, but I cannot agree with your methods of direct action"; who paternalistically believes he can set the timetable for another man's freedom; who lives by a mythical concept of time and who constantly advises the Negro to wait for a "more convenient season." Shallow understanding from people of good will is more frustrating than absolute misunderstanding from people of ill will. Lukewarm acceptance is much more bewildering than outright rejection.*

In other words, often times, it is the white moderate or the white exceptionalist who gets in the way of antiracism. Because they do not believe that they are a part of white supremacy, they do not see that they hold antiracism back by telling BIPOC to wait or change their activist tactics, and they think that having good intentions or giving lukewarm acceptance is the same as being antiracist.

HERE IS THE MOST IMPORTANT LESSON I WANT YOU TO UNDERSTAND ABOUT WHITE EXCEPTIONALISM.

❖ When people with white privilege believe they are exceptional when it comes to racism, they won't do the work of antiracism. If they do not do the work, they continue to do harm to BIPOC, even if that is not their intention.

❖ No person who has white privilege is exceptional, meaning they are not exempt from the conditioning of white supremacy, the benefits of white privilege, and the responsibility to keep practicing antiracism for the rest of their lives.

RECAP, REFLECT, RESPOND

RECAP

White exceptionalism is the belief that many people with white privilege often have about themselves that they are not racist, do not have racist thoughts, beliefs, or behaviors, and that they are "one of the good ones." They think that other white people are racist, but they aren't, and that they are excluded from the effects, benefits, and conditioning of white supremacy, so they do not have to do antiracism work.

REFLECT

❖ Read the extract from Martin Luther King Jr.'s letter again and think back on the topics we have covered so far in this book. How has white exceptionalism prevented people with white privilege from truly practicing antiracism? What do you think Martin Luther King Jr. would advise them to do instead?

❖ How have the white adults in your life (parents, caregivers, teachers, family members) unknowingly taught or practiced white exceptionalism? For example, have they taught you that as long as you are kind to people of all races, then that is being antiracist?

❖ In what ways have you witnessed people who have white privilege who are nice and kind still say or do things that are unknowingly racist?

❖ What do you now understand is the difference between being nice and being antiracist?

RESPOND

How People with White Privilege Can Respond to White Exceptionalism:

❖ Remember that racism and white supremacy are not about whether you are a good person or a bad person. If somebody tells you that something you've said or done is racist (and you didn't mean it to be!), remember that they are not saying that you are a bad person but rather that you've unknowingly done something that is racist. Instead of reacting with white exceptionalism or white fragility, use this as an opportunity to ask questions and learn more so you can better understand what happened and how not to cause more harm in the future.

❖ Remember that even if you are a nice and kind person who does your very best to be antiracist, you still benefit from white privilege and white supremacy and have the ability to purposely choose to be racist if you want to. Know that antiracism isn't about how many good things you do as an antiracist ally (which we'll cover in chapter 17) but instead about continuing to show up no matter what.

How People Who Don't Have White Privilege Can Respond to White Exceptionalism:

❖ Remember that there are people in your life who have white privilege who may be good, nice, and kind but who will still practice white exceptionalism. They often do it unknowingly and without bad intentions. However, that doesn't mean that it doesn't hurt or isn't racist. You have the right to let people know that their white exceptionalism is hurtful to you or others.

CHAPTER 11

check-in

Well done! You've learned an incredible amount so far!
Let's take a pause.

I know that we have covered a lot, so this is a great
time to stop and reflect on everything that we've learned
so far and how you are feeling.

Over the last ten chapters, you will have begun to
notice a pattern. All the white supremacy themes we
have covered weave in and out of each other, interlock-
ing and interconnecting. For example, white fragility
can sometimes show up as white silence. Tone policing
often comes from believing in white superiority. And
white privilege often leads to white exceptionalism.

This is something that you will continue to see as we go through this journey. This is the tricky, sticky web of white supremacy. It is not just the binary of you are either racist or you aren't. Instead, it is multilayered behaviors and beliefs that make up a white supremacist worldview (a worldview that white people are superior to people of other races).

As you read the theme for each chapter and completed the reflection questions, a lot of things will have come to the surface that you were probably not aware of before. You are now beginning to see that white supremacy and racism operate in very subtle ways during our everyday interactions. It's often not an obvious act like name-calling or excluding others (though this is racism too), but it's just the everyday ways we interact with each other and with the world.

THIS JOURNEY MAY HAVE BROUGHT UNCOMFORTABLE FEELINGS SUCH AS:

❖ Confusion or frustration
❖ Guilt or shame
❖ Anger
❖ Sadness
❖ Tiredness

While these feelings don't feel good, I want you to know that they are natural feelings to have on this journey. We are talking about some really difficult things, and it's not easy. It's painful to talk about racism—whether you have perpetuated it or been harmed by it. But I also want to remind you that you are not alone on this journey. There are many adults and young people who are taking this journey with you all around the world. And as we continue to learn more about white supremacy, you *will* come to a place of feeling empowered to combat racism and help change the world.

For now, though, I want you to take some time to process the feelings that this journey is bringing up for you.

HERE ARE SOME TIPS FOR HOW TO DO THAT:

❖ **NAME YOUR FEELINGS.** It's important to identify exactly what you are feeling so that you can honor those feelings and find ways to move through them. What exactly do you feel? Circle any of the words that best describe how you feel. Feel free to add your own feelings to the list too.

Sad	Bored	Sorry
Mad	Sick	Embarrassed
Angry	Thoughtful	Disgusted
Worried	Confused	Frustrated
Scared	Fed up	Helpless
Nervous	Hateful	Guilty
Annoyed	Lonely	Tired
Surprised	Overwhelmed	Ashamed
Upset	Curious	

❖ **ASK FOR HELP.** Talk to a trusted adult in your life about what you've been learning and how you are feeling. Ask them for help on how to move through these feelings. It would be especially helpful to talk to an adult who has read the adult version of *Me and White Supremacy*, because they'll know exactly how you are feeling.

❖ **CRY IT OUT.** If you are feeling emotions such as sadness, fear, or even anger, it's very helpful and healthy to cry them out. Whether you prefer to cry alone or with a trusted friend or adult, allow yourself to express your emotions through tears. It is much better to let it out than to bottle it up and keep it in.

❖ **WORK IT OUT.** One way to express strong emotions like anger is to work it out of your body through exercise or physical activity. Running, swimming, bike riding, yoga, dancing, team sports, or just punching a pillow are helpful ways to express anger without hurting yourself or others.

❖ **GIVE YOURSELF A TIME-OUT.** Do you know why parents sometimes give little kids a time-out? It's so that both the child and the parent can have a moment to calm down, think about their actions and feelings, and make better choices for their well-being. You might not be a little kid anymore, but giving ourselves a time-out can be one of the best things we can do for ourselves. A time-out means putting this book away for a few days or even more (if that's what you need) and allowing yourself the space to calm down, think about your actions and feelings, and make better antiracist choices for yourself and for others going forward. Meditation or other mindfulness practices are also a great way to give yourself a time-out. There is no rush. Give yourself the time you need.

❖ **AFFIRM YOURSELF.** Positive affirmations are true statements about ourselves that remind us of our goodness and our worthiness. When reading about white supremacy and doing the reflection questions in this book, you may have started to believe negative things about yourself, for example that you are bad or that you are a victim. These negative beliefs are harmful to us and are not what antiracism is about. Take some time to affirm the good things about yourself. Here are some positive affirmations that can help you. Say them to yourself whenever you notice yourself feeling bad.

I am a good person who is learning how to be better.

I am courageous.

I am safe and secure.

I am important.

I am smart.

I speak to myself with kindness.

It's okay to be angry/sad/scared.

I stand up for myself.

I am loved.

I can do hard things.

I forgive myself for my mistakes.

I learn from my mistakes.

I am strong.

It's okay to be vulnerable.

I can ask for help.

I like myself.

I believe in myself.

I can make a difference.

I matter.

I am a good friend.

I am proud of myself.

I love myself.

I am a leader.

I am using my voice to make a difference.

I am a change maker.

It's safe to express my feelings.

I have an open heart and an open mind.

I learn from my challenges.

I am becoming better every day.

CHAPTER 12

color blindness

When I was around six or seven years old, my teacher told our class that we would be performing a play for our parents. The play we would be performing was to be *Sleeping Beauty*. I was so excited! Like many of the girls in my class, I really wanted to be picked for the role of Princess Aurora. I loved the Disney movie and fantasized about being on stage as Sleeping Beauty herself.

However, as roles began to be handed out, my dream never materialized. I saw the role go to one of my classmates who looked exactly like Princess Aurora. She had fair white skin and golden blond hair, just like Sleeping Beauty herself. I, on the other hand, had brown skin and kinky Afro hair, and I was the only Black girl in my class. That was when I realized that I would *never* have been considered for the role of Sleeping Beauty. In fact, I would never be considered for the role of any Disney princess or any major protagonist in any books I read or TV shows and movies I watched. Growing up in the 1980s, Black girls were hardly ever represented in the media. And so there was no place for me to shine and be seen.

The role I was given was that of the mirror. My lines were in response to that famous line in the story: "Magic mirror on the wall, who's the fairest one of all?" I still remember how sad and angry I felt having to answer that the fairest one of all was not somebody who looked like me. I remember feeling invisible and that my only role in this world would be to reflect back to white people *their* beauty, instead of seeing and being celebrated *for my own*.

At age six or seven, I began to learn that there was no such thing as *color blindness*. I knew that white people saw the color of my skin and treated me differently because of it. I knew that the world we lived in was not color-blind. And I knew that white people, like my white teacher and classmates, didn't realize that.

WHAT IS COLOR BLINDNESS?

Have you ever said or heard the phrase *I don't see color* when you or someone else were talking about race? Have you ever thought it was rude or racist to talk about someone's race? Have you ever believed that the best way to solve racism was to ignore race and just focus on treating people equally? These are all examples of race-based color blindness.

Color blindness is the idea that you do not see someone's color and that you do not notice differences in race. Or if you do, that you do not treat people differently or discriminate against them based on those differences.

As a child, I could never understand why white parents would shush their children whenever they used the word *Black* to describe a Black person. "Don't say that! It's rude!" they would say in hushed tones, embarrassed that their child had said something that was apparently offensive. But what made it offensive? I *was* Black. This was an observation of difference (that I had a different skin color from them) and not a hateful comment. How were they supposed to refer to me? These parents sometimes took it a step further by saying things like, "They're not Black. They're just a person." What did this mean? And why was it so important for them not to say the word *Black*? It often left me wondering whether *Black* meant *bad*. Was my skin color a source of shame? And if so, was I expected to act as if I were not Black to make white people more comfortable around me?

Well-meaning parents and adults who have white privilege are often very uncomfortable talking about race and white supremacy with children and young people. As we discussed in chapter 6, most likely when they were young, their parents did not have meaningful conversations with them about race and white privilege and how to be antiracist. And so they grew up into adults who don't know how to talk about it without feeling really uncomfortable. They want to raise and teach children to not be racist, but they don't know the best way to do this.

SO INSTEAD THEY TEACH SIMPLE, WELL-INTENTIONED PRINCIPLES LIKE:

- ❖ We don't see color.
- ❖ We don't treat people differently because of the color of their skin.
- ❖ We do our best to treat everyone the same.

❖   We are color-blind.

❖   Talking about race is racist or creates racism.

❖   The best way to fight racism is to ignore race.

These may seem like good principles to practice. However, they don't work because science and society won't let them.

The *Sleeping Beauty* story I shared at the beginning of this chapter is an example of racialization. Although nobody in the class told me that I couldn't be Sleeping Beauty because of my skin color, my classmates and I were all indirectly being taught that Black people are minorities that will receive fewer opportunities and that it is the norm that the heroes and heroines of stories should be white.

As much as adults with white privilege may tell young people not to be racist, to treat everyone equally, and to be color-blind, the truth is that both science and society continue to uphold racism whether we like it or not. So when adults teach young people to be color-blind, they are not teaching them the best way to be antiracist.

HOW DOES COLOR BLINDNESS SHOW UP?

Some common color blind statements are:

❖ I don't see color. I only see people.

❖ I don't even see you as Black!

❖ I don't care if a person is black, white, green, yellow, purple, or blue!

❖ He/she/they are a Person of Color (when referring to a Black person, because saying "Black" makes them feel uncomfortable).

❖ I don't think that bad thing happened to you because you're a Person of Color. I've experienced something like that before, and I'm white (in response to a Person of Color sharing their lived experience of racism).

ASK YOURSELF

• What messages have you been taught about color blindness by parents and teachers?

• How have you noticed people with white privilege reacting when they have to talk about "seeing color" (that is, when they have to talk about race, especially about being white)?

• Do any of the behaviors we've talked about so far show up, such as white fragility or tone policing? Why do you think that is?

SCIENCE

A popular belief is that racism is something that is actively taught to people and that if parents don't purposely teach their children to be racist, then they won't be racist. However, science says the opposite. Extensive scientific studies have shown that babies notice race-based differences from as early as six months old and that by three to five years old, children are already internalizing racial biases. Of course, this is not because children believe in racism or white superiority! It's because their brains are sorting out the world, trying to make sense of it all, and using societal messages to categorize things and people.

SOCIETY

Society is constantly feeding us messages about race, through a process called *racialization*. Racialization is a process by which we attach racial meaning, identities, behaviors, stereotypes, and roles to people of different races. In other words, it's a process through which we learn what it means to be our race and what it means to be other races in this society. Racialization happens at home, at school, in the neighborhood, with family, friends, and peer groups, on TV and in movies, at shops and stores, in books and plays, in art and music, through social media, and so on. Racialization teaches us that white people are "normal" people or "race-less" people and BIPOC are "other" people and have a race.

WHY DO WE NEED TO LOOK AT COLOR BLINDNESS?

Color blindness may seem like a good way to solve racism, but the truth is that it doesn't work. As human beings, we are not racially color-blind. We do notice when people are different from us, whether it is skin complexion, hair, facial features, or culture. Our brains are biologically wired to notice differences and then to sort things into categories based on those differences. And because we live in a world where white supremacy is the dominant culture, we then assign superiority and inferiority to those groups of people depending on the lightness or darkness of their skin.

When people say that they are color-blind, they are often trying to do the right thing, but they are going about it the wrong way. The best way to combat racism *is* to notice race. This means being color conscious instead of color-blind. When we are color conscious, we are aware of our differences and we honor them. We don't sort people into categories of superiority and inferiority; instead we acknowledge and celebrate all the different ways that human beings look and how complex all human cultures are. Most importantly, when we are color conscious, we accept that we live in a world that treats people differently based on their race. We don't pretend that racism doesn't exist. We accept that it does exist and that some people hold racial privileges while others do not. We admit that we currently live in a world where not everyone is treated the same, and we do our best to help change it.

If my teacher and classmates had told me that they were color-blind when I was young, I would not have believed them. And I would have been very upset that they were denying that my race and my racial experiences were not real, when I knew very well that there were experiences I was being denied because of the color of my skin. If I could talk to that teacher now, I would tell her that I wish she could have acknowledged that she was not color-blind, that she did see my race, that she did treat me differently because of it, and that I wished she would have had conversations about race, difference, and privilege in the class so that I would have felt seen and acknowledged for my experiences as a Black girl. Talking about race would not have been racist; it would have been antiracist.

RECAP, REFLECT, RESPOND

RECAP

Color blindness is the idea that you do not see some-one's color, that you do not notice differences in race, or if you do, that you do not treat people differently or oppress people based on those differences.

REFLECT

❖ How do you think having a color-blind attitude harms BIPOC?

❖ Racialization often classes white people as being race-less, but socially speaking, white people are a race too. What do you think it means to be white? What does society tell us about what it means to be white?

❖ Racialization often classes BIPOC as being differ-ent, other, or minorities who are not the norm. What do you think it means to be a BIPOC? What does society tell us about what it means to be a BIPOC?

RESPOND

How People with White Privilege Can Respond to Color Blindness:

❖ Choose to be color conscious instead of color-blind.

It's important for us to see color. It's important to celebrate our differences and acknowledge that we live in a society that attaches superiority or inferiority to people based on the color of their skin.

❖ When you become color conscious, you become more aware of the injustices of racism. Use color consciousness to speak up about racism and advocate for people to practice antiracism.

❖ When watching TV or movies, attending musicals, and reading books, pay attention to racialization. Which fictional or nonfictional figures are seen as the norm, and which are seen as other or minorities? Who are cast as the heroes and heroines, and who are cast as the villains? Who are often the protagonists? Does color blindness really exist in these spaces?

How People Who Don't Have White Privilege Can Respond to Color Blindness:

❖ Acknowledge and celebrate your own race and those of other BIPOC. Racialization often teaches us that to be BIPOC is to be inferior to white people. However, you are not inferior; you are the same. Have pride in who you are, what you look like, where you come from, your history, and your culture. Do not be color-blind to yourself.

❖ When people tell you that they are color-blind or that they don't see you as the color you are, share with them what you've learned in this chapter. Explain that while they may think that color blindness is a good thing, it's actually harmful because it ignores your unique differences and ignores the fact that you experience racism. Encourage them to become color conscious,

❖ When watching TV or movies, attending musicals, and reading books, pay attention to racialization. Which fictional or nonfictional figures are seen as the norm, and which are seen as other or minorities? Who are cast as the heroes and heroines, and who are cast as the villains? Who are often the protagonists? Does color blindness really exist in these spaces?

CHAPTER 13

anti-blackness

When I was a kid, I often wondered why my mother was so focused on me and my brothers being high achievers and top students at school. She didn't want us to just do well; she wanted us to outshine every other student in our classes. Luckily for me, I've always loved learning and still do to this day. But the pressure to always be at the top of the class was tough.

As an adult and a mother myself now, I can see how daunting it must have been for her raising Black Muslim children in a society that was anti-Black. Especially as a Black mother raising children alone while my dad worked away at sea many months of the year. I was born and grew up in a society that treated Black people and immigrants as if we were less intelligent, less civilized, and less worthy of accomplishment and success than everyone else.

My mother often tells us about our childhood, "I wanted you to be the best!" My parents have both always strived for excellence, but when I think back on my mother's words, I also think that what she meant is that she didn't want any white person to have a reason to pigeonhole us or treat us badly. She didn't want them to limit my brothers and me to what they saw Black people as being capable and worthy of. She wanted to bullet-proof and supercharge us through academic success, because she understood very well how white supremacy treats Black children and Black people. She understood *anti-Blackness*.

WHAT IS ANTI-BLACKNESS?

Merriam-Webster defines *anti-Black* as "opposed to or hostile toward Black people," and the Movement for Black Lives defines *anti-Black racism* as a "term used to specifically describe the unique discrimination, violence, and harms imposed on and impacting Black people specifically."

In short, anti-Blackness is the specific racism that is experienced by Black people and people of African descent around the world. At the beginning of this book, we explored the historical roots of white supremacist ideology through the European thinkers and scientists who grouped people into different "races" and gave them different attributes—with themselves being the "most supreme" race. We saw how this scientific racism was used to justify colonizing countries around the world, including all across the continent of Africa, and how this colonization including kidnapping, enslaving, and selling African people for violent slave labor.

As white supremacy defines white people as the "most supreme" race, it simultaneously defines Black people as the "most inferior" race. Of course, none of these ideas are true in any way. However, white-dominant society continues to play out these tropes, even though we now live in the twenty-first century.

Another important thing to understand about anti-Blackness is that it is not just a type of racism that white people commit. It's also, sadly, something that non-Black People of Color can commit against Black people too. And even further, it's a type of racism that Black people can internalize against themselves and against each other. This is because white supremacy has so powerfully conditioned us all to view being Black as being the worst thing you can be. It gives Black people the least societal privileges and the most violent forms of oppression around the world, with darker-skinned Black people generally experiencing this to even greater degrees. Anti-Blackness therefore becomes a strange and very harmful thing that people consciously or unconsciously participate in to try to protect themselves from the consequences of being Black in white supremacy's eyes.

Another strange component to this is that being Black is also often seen as being cool in our society. From Black celebrities to Black music, Black sports people, viral TikTok dances by Black creators, funny Black GIFs, Black slang, "Blaccents" (Black accents), Black hairstyles, skin tones, and facial features, and so on, Black culture undeniably defines popular culture. However, this so-called admiration of Blackness doesn't mean that anti-Black racism doesn't exist. We'll talk about cultural appropriation soon, but for now it's important to understand that loving Black culture and having Black friends and family members does not protect non-Black people from anti-Black racism.

HOW DOES ANTI-BLACKNESS SHOW UP?

Anti-Blackness shows up differently from Black babies to Black children to Black adults, becoming progressively more harmful and even violent as Black people grow up.

BLACK BABIES

Anti-Blackness begins to affect Black people before they are even born. Because of the way Black mothers are treated by largely white medical institutions and practitioners, they are three to four times more likely to die from pregnancy-and-childbirth-related causes than their white counterparts in the United States and five times more likely in the United Kingdom. This is called the Black maternal health crisis, and it directly affects the number of Black children who get to grow up and be parented by their mothers, which has implications for their quality of life.

When Black people are babies, they are often seen as cute and adorable. Cute brown babies with cute curly hair. Some (not all!) non-Black people even want to have Black or biracial babies just because they see them as so cute. This is called exoticization, where some non-Black people fantasize about how exotic it would be to have a baby who is so different and other from themselves.

And sometimes it's the opposite, where non-Black people absolutely do not want to have children who are Black or biracial, because they see a Black child as being less worthy of their love. In 2021, Prince Harry of the British royal family and his wife Meghan Markle, the Duchess of Sussex, gave an interview with Oprah Winfrey where they shared the shocking revelation that when Meghan, who is biracial, was pregnant with her first child, Archie, concerns were raised by a member of the royal family about the baby's potentially darker skin complexion.

BLACK CHILDREN

As Black children get older, anti-Blackness begins to show up in even greater ways. Some recent U.S. studies show how Black children experience something called "adultification," which is where Black children are seen as and treated as though they are actually older than they are. A 2014 study called "The Essence of Innocence: Consequences of Dehumanizing Black Children" found that from the age of ten, Black boys are perceived as older and more likely to be guilty than their white peers and that police violence against them is seen as more justified. We only have to look at African American boys like Tamir Rice and Trayvon Martin, who were killed because they were perceived not as a twelve-year-old and a seventeen-year-old, but instead as grown adult men.

A 2017 study called "Girlhood Interrupted: The Erasure of Black Girls' Childhood" found that Black girls in the age range of five to fourteen were seen as less innocent and more adult than their white peers.

THE STUDY SHOWED THAT ADULTS
VIEWED BLACK GIRLS AS FOLLOWS:

❖ Black girls need less nurturing.

❖ Black girls need less protection.

❖ Black girls need to be supported less.

❖ Black girls need to be comforted less.

❖ Black girls are more independent.

❖ Black girls know more about adult topics.

❖ Black girls know more about sex.

Additionally, the study showed that because of this adultification, Black girls received harsher punishments by educators and school resource officers, fewer leadership and mentoring opportunities in schools, and greater use of force and harsher penalties in the juvenile system.

Anti-Blackness can be even more harmful to Black people who identify as LGBTQIA+ because of the intersection of their other identities where they also experience discrimination.

Similarly, anti-Blackness against Black girls and women is intensified because of the discrimination they also experience due to their gender. African American feminist scholar, writer, and activist Moya Bailey coined the term *misogynoir* to describe what she calls "the particular brand of hatred directed at Black women in American visual and popular culture."

BLACK ADULTS

By the time Black people are adults, they have been on the receiving end of direct and indirect anti-Black racism for many years, whether they realize it or not. The negative stereotypes and tropes of Black people get progressively more negative as they become actual adults.

Black adults are often perceived as more angry, strong, aggressive, wild, and threatening than white adults. If Black adults express emotions like frustration, they are often seen as attacking others. If they are quiet or prefer to keep to themselves, they are often seen as unfriendly or arrogant. If they are sad or upset, they are often seen as manipulative. If they enjoy hobbies and activities that are not perceived as "Black" or don't talk in ways that are perceived as "Black," then they are called Oreos (in other words, Black on the outside, white on the inside) or told "you're not really Black." When they get into positions of leadership and authority, people are often surprised, sometimes even confused. After all, we still continue to see titles like "the first Black XYZ" when a Black person receives an accolade that has historically been granted to white people. At work, Black adults are paid less than their white counterparts and receive fewer opportunities for progress and promotion. (This explains why my mother worked so hard to get us to be academically excellent—she knew how much was working against us.) When Black adults try to protest against racism, they are criticized for "pulling the race card" or, like Colin Kaepernick, punished for using their voice and their platform to fight injustice.

In the United States, there is of course a fraught and abusive relationship between Black people and the justice system. The violent killings of thousands of Black people at the hands of the police, some globally known like George Floyd and Breonna Taylor and some whose names we'll never get to hear but whose lives also matter, are directly correlated to anti-Blackness. Anti-Blackness often has a profound effect both on how Black people live and how they die.

ASK YOURSELF:

- If you are Black, how have you noticed anti-Blackness impacting you and your Black friends and family?
- If you are not Black, how have you noticed anti-Blackness impacting Black people in your community?
- If you are Black biracial or mixed race, how have you seen anti-Blackness impacting you and/or impacting the way you interact with other Black people?

WHY DO WE NEED TO LOOK AT ANTI-BLACKNESS?

In 2020, we saw one of the largest global protests of our time. Ignited by the killings of Breonna Taylor, Ahmaud Arbery, George Floyd, among many others, Black Lives Matter protests across the United States and around the world took the world by storm as people of all races demanded justice and equity for Black people. But these protests didn't just come out of nowhere. Black Lives Matter itself was founded in 2013, after the acquittal of George Zimmerman in the shooting death of African American teen Trayvon Martin. For centuries, Black people have been protesting, marching, and organizing to fight anti-Black racism and discrimination, which is why it is important for us to explore anti-Blackness in depth on this journey.

Fighting anti-Blackness is
fighting white supremacy.

The statement "Black Lives Matter" does not mean that Black lives matter *more* than other people's lives. It means, as this chapter has shown, that white supremacy and anti-Black racism treat Black people as if they matter *less* than everybody else. Affirming that Black Lives Matter is affirming that Black people matter too. Black people matter the same as everyone else, and society needs to change to reflect that.

RECAP, REFLECT, RESPOND

RECAP

Anti-Blackness is the specific racism that is experienced by Black people and people of African descent around the world. It is defined by Merriam-Webster as being opposed to or hostile toward Black people.

REFLECT

* What are some anti-Black stereotypes you have seen in movies and on TV? Are Black people often given specific roles such as the sassy sidekick, the villain, or the magical helper? Why do you think that is?

* Why do you think that the majority of protagonist roles don't go to Black actors?

* How have you noticed Black children are treated by white adults such as neighbors, teachers, and shop employees?

* How have you noticed Black adults are treated by businesses and police officers?

* How do you think the world would positively change for all people if the idea of white supremacy and Black inferiority disappeared today?

RESPOND

How Non-Black People Can Respond to Anti-Blackness:

❖ Challenge anti-Black racism whenever you witness it. Whether it's someone being called the N-word or an Oreo, call it out and let people know that their actions are anti-Black. Help to educate them on how not to perpetuate anti-Black racism.

❖ Think about some of the things that you have said or thought about Black people that were knowingly or unknowingly racist. Think about where you learned these thoughts and how they were harmful to the people they were directed at. Make a commitment to challenge your own anti-Blackness going forward.

❖ Remember that liking Black people or having Black friends or even family members doesn't mean that anti-Blackness doesn't exist in your thoughts or behaviors. Remember that even if you didn't consciously choose these thoughts, they are there because we live in a world that is constantly reinforcing anti-Blackness to us. It's not about whether you are a good person or a bad person, whether you are racist or not racist. It's about educating yourself so that you can actively practice antiracism.

❖ If you are a non-Black Person of Color, experiencing racism yourself does not give you an excuse or a reason to be racist to Black people. Instead, it should be a reason to join forces with Black people to fight white supremacy.

How Black People Can Respond to Anti-Blackness:

❖ Challenge anti-Black racism whenever you see it. Whether it's someone being called the N-word or an Oreo, call it out and let people know that their actions are anti-Black. Help to educate them on how not to perpetuate anti-Black racism.

❖ Remember that anti-Blackness is also something that Black people can internalize against themselves and other Black people. This can look like colorism, where darker-skinned Black people experience more prejudice and discrimination than lighter-skinned Black people. It can also look like having a low sense of self-esteem and confidence because deep down inside, you believe white supremacy's lie that we are inferior. I want to remind you that it is a *lie*, and the truth is that being who *you* uniquely are is the greatest gift.

CHAPTER 14

racist stereotypes

Like many kids, I grew up watching Disney movies. *Dumbo*, *Peter Pan*, *Lady and the Tramp*, and *Aladdin* were just a few of the movies I remember watching as a little girl in the 1980s and 1990s. Of course, we didn't have streaming platforms like Disney+ back then! So we would watch them on videotapes or if they happened to be playing on TV. I remember being mesmerized by the stories and dancing along to the songs. And I still love watching Disney movies to this day, like *Coco*, *Moana*, and *Soul*, now with my own kids, and definitely on Disney+!

What I didn't realize back then but definitely

recognize now as an adult is how many of these movies reinforced negative stereotypes about people of different races. *Dumbo*, for example, has a group of characters who are crows who are friendly toward the young elephant. The crows, however, are racist caricatures of Black Americans. Peter Pan has a friend named Tiger Lily who belongs to a Native American tribe. Sadly, the tribe speaks in gibberish rather than an actual indigenous language and even sing an offensive song called "What Made the Red Man Red." In *Lady and the Tramp*, the character Aunt Sarah has two Siamese cats who are depicted as racist caricatures of Asian people with bucked teeth, slanted eyes, and stereotypical East Asian accents. In *Aladdin*, the opening song, "Arabian Nights," has the line, "Where they cut off your ear if they don't like your face / It's barbaric, but hey, it's home." This is a stereotypically racist depiction of Arabs as barbaric savages. And the list goes on and on.

In 2020, Disney+ made the decision to tackle this problem of negative racist stereotypes in their movies head-on. They now include a disclaimer at the beginning of some of these titles that says, "This program includes negative depictions and/or mistreatment of people or cultures. These stereotypes were wrong then and are wrong now. Rather than remove this content, we want to acknowledge its harmful impact, learn from it, and spark conversation to create a more inclusive future together."

This is an important and necessary step in the right direction to tackling how the media and movies perpetuate racism. Racist stereotypes are taught to children through movies from a very young age and go on to negatively impact how they see themselves and people of other backgrounds as they grow up.

WHAT ARE RACIST STEREOTYPES?

We spent the last chapter looking at anti-Blackness, which is how white supremacy and racism specifically impacts Black people. In this chapter, we are going to explore how white supremacy impacts Indigenous people and People of Color.

A racist stereotype is a negative depiction of a wide group of people belonging to one race or

Oxford Languages defines a stereotype as "a widely held but fixed and oversimplified image or idea of a particular type of person or thing."

ethnicity that reinforces the idea that they are inferior, other, and not civilized in the way white people are, with white people being the standard of what is considered "normal." Racist stereotypes trap people in boxes as flat, one-dimensional characters rather than allowing them to be the complex, unique, interesting human beings they truly are. Racist stereotypes make implicit and explicit statements, like "Arabs are terrorists" and "Asians are smart," rather than recognizing that Arab people and Asian people are billions of people with different personalities, passions, and perspectives. Racist stereotypes trap whole groups of people into being just one or two things.

PREJUDICE VS. RACISM

You may be thinking that white people also have to deal with racist stereotypes from BIPOC, such as white women being called "Karens" and white men being called "Brads" in stereotypically negative ways. This is where it's important to understand the difference between prejudice and racism.

Prejudice + Power = Racism

WHAT IS PREJUDICE?

All people, regardless of race, are capable of being prejudiced toward people who are not the same race as them. A person of any race can *prejudge* a person of any other race based on negative racial stereotypes and other factors. Prejudice is wrong, because it paints a large group of people with a single brush, but it's not the same as racism.

WHAT IS RACISM?

Racism occurs when *prejudice* is combined with *power*. Racism occurs when the dominant racial group (which, in a white supremacist society, is people with white privilege) is able to dominate over all other racial groups and negatively affect those racial groups at all levels—interpersonally, institutionally, and structurally.

Though a BIPOC can hold prejudice against a white person by calling them Karen or Brad, they cannot be racist toward a white person. They do not have the *power* (which comes with white privilege) and the backing of a system of oppression (called white supremacy) to be able to turn that prejudice into domination and punishment in a way that a white person would be able to do if the tables were reversed.

BIPOC might use prejudice to call white people names, which is wrong. But white people can use their prejudice and power to get BIPOC kept out of positions of leadership and influence, fired from their jobs, and even arrested and/or killed by police officers. It's just not the same.

HOW DO RACIST STEREOTYPES SHOW UP?

As we talked about at the beginning of this chapter, racist stereotypes are taught to us from an early age through children's movies, and reinforced to us over and over again every day through books, TV shows, music videos, social media, the news, advertisements, and even things we are taught at school.

Below is a list of broad groups of people by race and ethnicity.

❖ Asian people
❖ Latinx people
❖ Indigenous people
❖ Arab people

On the next page is a list of negative racial stereotypes. Take a look at the two lists and see if you can match up which stereotypes are usually given to which groups of people. Take a moment to think about where you learned these stereotypes and who you usually hear saying them.

Poor	Aggressive
Lazy	Overachieving
Less educated	Good at martial arts
Less intelligent	Helpless
Exotic	Rich
Job stealing	Gang members
Ghetto	Scary
Spicy	Smart
Wild	Savages
Spiritual	Barbarians
Mystical	Strong
Sexist	Weak
Oppressed	Nerds
Primitive	Dirty
Terrorists	Criminals
Drug dealers	Illegal

WHILE YOU LOOK AT RACIST STEREOTYPES WITHIN THESE GROUPS, KEEP THESE THINGS IN MIND:

Each group in this list covers many countries, nations, and cultures, each with its own rich and complex history—both with white supremacy and colonialism and with one another.

The groups we are looking at here are very broad and include within themselves many subgroups that are affected in different ways by white supremacy. For example, in the group of people broadly called Asians, white supremacy impacts them in different ways depending on whether they are South Asian, East Asian, Southeast Asian, or Pacific Islanders. They may be even further impacted by their immigration status, for example being born a citizen vs. being an immigrant vs. being undocumented.

Religions are not races. However, racial groups often experience religious prejudice and discrimination associated with certain racial groups, regardless of whether they observe that particular religion or even belong to that particular religion. For example, though the group of people broadly called Arabs belong to diverse religions, non-Muslim Arabs can experience Islamophobic stereotypes because of the media-driven idea in films and the news that all Muslims are Arabs and all Arabs are terrorists.

You can belong to a group that experiences racial stereotypes and oppression while still holding white privilege or white-passing privilege. Being one thing doesn't cancel the other things that we also are but rather reminds us that we are both/and, not either/or.

Colorism is very important to keep in mind. Darker-skinned people often experience more racism than lighter-skinned people.

Just because a stereotype seems positive does not mean it is not harmful. Stereotypes rob people of their complex individuality and erase the impact that colonization has had on why some of these stereotypes have emerged in the first place.

WHY DO WE NEED TO LOOK AT RACIST STEREOTYPES?

Racist stereotypes continue to reinforce the idea that those who do not hold white privilege should not be given that privilege because they are other, inferior, and a threat to white civilization.

Racist stereotypes are used by politicians, policy makers, and the press to justify why certain groups of people should be treated the way that they are. It is easy to blame those in positions in leadership who drive racist stereotype narratives. But what about the narratives *we* hold that continue to make it acceptable to allow people from other races to be talked about and treated the way they are?

Although stereotypes are ridiculous when we say them out loud, because we are so used to them as "normal" ways of thinking about people, we don't realize just how much harm they are doing. Though most of us would never consciously choose to believe in these stereotypes or say them out loud, they do live inside us, because society keeps reinforcing them. And when people who have white privilege use these stereotypes with the power they have, it becomes a dangerous combination.

If subconsciously we believe that Indigenous people are primitive or Latinx people are criminals, then in some weird way, it makes sense to us when we see them being treated badly by the educational system, the justice system, the healthcare system, the immigration system, the employment system, and so on. Uncovering the racist stereotypes we hold can help us to actively fight against white supremacy.

RECAP, REFLECT, RESPOND

RECAP

Racist stereotypes are negative depictions of wide groups of people who belong to one race or ethnicity. They reinforce the idea that these groups of people are inferior, other, and not civilized in the way white people are, with white people being the standard of what is considered "normal."

REFLECT

❖ What are some racial stereotypes that are popular in your country—implicit and explicit, historic and modern—associated with Indigenous people and non-Black POC?

❖ How do you think POC who are citizens in your country are seen differently from those who are recent immigrants and those who are undocumented? For example, are they more likely to be painted with a racial stereotype if they have an accent from their own country? Why do you think that is?

❖ How do you think Indigenous children and non-Black children of color are treated differently from white children because of racist stereotypes?

RESPOND

❖ Challenging racist stereotypes in society starts with challenging the racist stereotypes we hold within our own minds first. Look back at the stereotypes matching activity and think about what it is about these stereotypes that you believe and why. This isn't about shaming yourself or feeling guilty. Instead it's about shining a light on the ways you might be contributing to racist stereotyping without even realizing it.

❖ Challenge other people who make jokes or untrue statements that use racist stereotypes. Racist jokes are not funny, and untrue statements are dangerous. If you have white privilege, this is where you make sure to challenge white silence.

❖ When watching movies and TV shows and reading books, pay attention to where racist stereotypes are being used. It's often quite subtle, such as the Asian kid in a story being a nerd or the Latina woman in a movie having a fiery personality. Think about how we might rewrite the story to make these characters more believable as three-dimensional human beings rather than one-dimensional caricatures.

CHAPTER 15

cultural appropriation

In November 2013, pop star Katy Perry took the stage at the American Music Awards to perform her new song "Unconditionally" as the opening act for the event. Wearing a modified dress that was part Japanese kimono and part Chinese cheongsam, heavy white "geisha-style" makeup, and a traditional Japanese hairstyle and hair ornaments, Perry belted out her song about unconditional love. She performed on a "Japanese-themed" stage with a troop of backup dancers who were similarly dressed as geishas. As she sang her song, they danced, bowed, and shuffled with Asian oil-paper umbrellas against the background of a beautiful Japanese garden.

Perry was quickly called out by critics for appropriating Japanese culture, but her response was that she was trying to pay homage to Japanese culture, as it was a culture that she loved.

A few months later, she released a video for her new song, "Dark Horse," in which she appeared as a female Egyptian pharaoh. Once again, she received some criticism for her appropriation and *exotification* of Egyptian culture.

A few months after that, she released a video for another new song, "This Is How We Do," in which her hair is styled in cornrows, with gelled-down baby hair, and she speaks with a Blaccent (Black accent) at one point and sings the line, "Now we're talking astrology, getting our nails did all Japanese-y." Once again, she received criticism for engaging in cultural appropriation.

EXOTIFICATION:

- The act of seeing someone or something from a different background or identity as being exotic, unusual, strange, mysterious, and "other." Racial exotification involves romanticizing different stereotypes about a different culture, and it arose from white Western Europeans colonizing nonwhite cultures and countries. In the examples shared here, Katy Perry exotified Asian and Black cultures in her music videos to create images of romanticized beauty, magic, and cool.

It wasn't until 2017, in an interview with African American activist and podcaster DeRay Mckesson, that Perry shared regret for her past acts of cultural appropriation and acknowledged her own white privilege in not understanding the significance of what she was doing. In the interview, she shared that she did not realize the significance of cornrows until her stylist, Cleo Wade, explained the history of Black hair culture and that, "Even in my intention to appreciate Japanese culture, I did it wrong with a performance... And I didn't know that I did it wrong until I heard people saying I did it wrong."

Perry explained that she did not understand, despite the criticism she received at the time, that by wearing and performing in clothes and hairstyles from non-white cultures, she was participating in acts of *cultural appropriation*.

WHAT IS CULTURAL APPROPRIATION?

In order to better understand **cultural appropriation**, let's first break down what the two words mean.

WHAT IS CULTURE?
* Culture is a broad umbrella term that encompasses the beliefs, behaviors, social norms and forms, and material traits of a racial, religious, or social group. Culture includes many things including a group's cultural objects, motifs, symbols, rituals, artifacts, and customs. Culture can be physical things, such as clothing, art, music, foods, literature, stories, religious customs, beauty practices, accessories, and so on. It can also be nonphysical things, such as ways of thinking, behaving, and even talking.

WHAT IS APPROPRIATION?

- To appropriate something is to take or use something without the right to do so.

The most basic definition of cultural appropriation therefore is that it is the act of taking or using something from another culture without the right to do so, because that cultural element does not belong to your culture.

However, the definition of cultural appropriation goes deeper than that. Every day in hundreds of ways, we use or engage with something from a different culture that is not our own. We eat foods from different cultures. We listen to music from different cultures. We speak languages from different cultures. *Are these acts also a type of cultural appropriation?*

Additionally, one person from a racial group can think something is culturally appropriative while another person from that same group can disagree and think that it isn't. For example, in 2013, Selena Gomez was accused by some people of appropriating South Asian culture when she wore a bindi, a traditional colored dot worn on the forehead, when performing at the

MTV Movie Awards. However, when asked about it in an interview at the time, Bollywood actress Priyanka Chopra said that she felt it was an act of embracing her culture rather than insulting it. *Is it still an act of cultural appropriation if someone from that culture doesn't believe it is?*

Questions such as these are what make understanding and discussing cultural appropriation so challenging. There is not one definition of cultural appropriation, not one list of what is and isn't culturally appropriative, and no single authority on whether something is an insult or an homage to a particular culture.

However, what is often missing from discussions about cultural appropriation is a deeper understanding of the impact of history, power, and dominance between the two cultures being discussed. Ijeoma Oluo, the author of the bestselling book *So You Want to Talk About Race*, offers a definition of cultural appropriation that is very helpful to these discussions. She defines cultural appropriation as "the adoption or exploitation of another culture by a more dominant culture."

According to this definition, the most important thing we need to understand is that it occurs between a *dominant* culture and a *nondominant* or *marginalized* culture. A dominant culture is one that has historically harmed and oppressed another culture through acts of colonization, land theft, mass kidnapping and enslavement, attempted genocide, forced assimilation, segregation, legalized racial discrimination, and the reinforcement of negative stereotypes. The dominant culture benefited from this oppression, and the nondominant or marginalized culture suffered as a result of it.

HERE ARE TWO EXAMPLES OF DOMINANT AND NONDOMINANT OR MARGINALIZED CULTURES WHERE CULTURAL APPROPRIATION OFTEN HAPPENS:

1. White, western Europeans colonized the lands now known as the Americas and Canada. White people systematically wiped out large numbers of Indigenous populations through disease and murder. They stole their lands and resources, confined them to small reservations, forcibly enrolled their children in boarding schools that stripped them of their cultures and connections to their families, and traumatized them through abuse. They deprived them of the privileges of health, safety, economic gain, and the same protections afforded to white citizens. They also ascribed

negative racist stereotypes to them and erased or rewrote the history of what they did to them.

At the same time, over the years, white people have appropriated and used different cultural elements from Indigenous people such as their traditional religious customs, practices, and clothing. They have used them without permission, changed their meanings and significance, sold them and therefore made money from things they took away from Indigenous people, and made themselves look cool, trendy, or exotic by engaging in them. Some common examples of this are wearing Native headdresses as Halloween costumes, dream catchers, calling things or people their "spirit animal," and using tribal name or images as mascots for sports teams.

2. Between 1858 to 1947, the British Crown took and enforced colonialist control over the Indian subcontinent. Prior to that, from the eighteenth century, large parts of the Indian subcontinent had been dominated by the British East India Company. For centuries, the British decimated the region's cultures and economies through exploitation, forced starvation, segregation, imprisonment, taxation, and forced labor. They enforced their language,

religion, and laws, and when independence was eventually won after decades of violent struggle, the British left the region in a state of utter devastation and disrepair. The British similarly ascribed negative racist stereotypes to the people of that region, and erased and rewrote the history of what they did to them. When Indian, Pakistani, Bangladeshi, and other people of South Asian descent emigrated to the United Kingdom, they faced racist violence and discrimination. They were also forced to downplay and be ashamed of their own culture, and to embrace and assimilate into British culture.

Despite discriminating against South Asian individuals, British people and white people around the world use and appropriate elements of South Asian culture including bindis and jewelry (nose rings, toe rings, anklets), profit from teaching yoga while disconnecting it from its spiritual roots, get tattoos of Hindu gods and goddesses, and adapt traditional South Asian fashion into "festival wear." The very things that South Asian people were and often still are mocked and ridiculed for are now used by white people to make themselves look spiritual, mystical, and exotic.

These are just two examples of how cultural appropriation shows up. But as you can imagine, as European countries partially or totally colonized almost every country in the world, and as white privilege is a form of dominance and power, cultural appropriation shows up everywhere white people interact with nonwhite people.

But does that mean that cultural appropriation is *always* happening when white people and nonwhite people are interacting? Are white people the *only* people who can culturally appropriate? And can BIPOC culturally appropriate from white people?

THESE ARE GREAT QUESTIONS TO EXPLORE!

❖ Is cultural appropriation always happening when white people and nonwhite people are interacting?

⬦ Cultural appropriation is about exploitation, the reinforcement of racist stereotypes and anti-Blackness, and the upholding of white supremacy. The other side of the coin of cultural appropriation is cultural appreciation. But appreciation is not just about holding the intent to appreciate (like Katy Perry believed she was doing). It also requires the following:

◆ Deeply studying and understanding the

cultural or spiritual significance of the cultural element you are seeking to use

- Not financially benefiting from that cultural element, but instead sharing or redirecting any money you make to people of the culture that the element belongs to

- Understanding the historical context of colonialism and racism between your culture and that culture

- Not using that cultural element as a costume or something to make yourself look cool, but instead using it in the context that it is intended. There is a big difference between wearing a traditional Asian dress at an Asian wedding versus wearing it on a stage as a costume for a music performance that has nothing to do with Asia.

❖ Are white people the only people who can culturally appropriate?

◇ Nonwhite people can absolutely culturally appropriate from other nonwhite cultures, even if there has not been a relationship of dominance and nondominance between the two countries. For example, in 2016, Beyoncé was called out for appropriating Indian culture in her music video for "Hymn for the Weekend" with Coldplay. Again, there are people of Indian descent who see this video as an example of cultural appropriation and others who see it is an example of cultural appreciation. My personal feeling is that when we use elements of another culture as a costume, for entertainment, for economic gain, or even just because we think it makes us look cool, we are veering into cultural appropriation and should be wary.

❖ Can BIPOC culturally appropriate from white people?

✧ If it's culturally appropriative for white people to dress as Pocahontas, a Mexican, an Arab, or a Native American or wear blackface makeup to dress up as a Black person, does that mean it's also culturally appropriative for BIPOC to dress as Sleeping Beauty, Elsa, Captain Marvel, Iron Man, or another white fictional or historical person? The answer to this is no, it is not the same. This is because white people have never been collectively colonized, racially discriminated against, or harmed because they are white. They have never been conditioned to be ashamed of white culture or been ridiculed for the way they dress, eat, talk, worship, or look. BIPOC may straighten their curly or coily hair out of preference, but they have also for centuries been systemically discriminated against for how their hair naturally grows out of their heads. The reverse is not true.

HOW DOES CULTURAL APPROPRIATION SHOW UP?

Cultural appropriation shows up in a number of different spheres, including but not limited to the following:

❖ **FASHION:** the appropriation of cultural fashion styles, usually by white designers appropriating from BIPOC, and often without credit or attribution to the original culture. For example, fashion brands Zara, Anthropologie, and Patowl have been accused by Mexico's Ministry of Culture of appropriating patterns from indigenous Mexican groups in some of their clothing designs without any credit or benefit to those communities.

❖ **HAIR:** the appropriation of traditionally African heritage hairstyles worn on non-Black people. For example,

Justin Bieber wearing locs and the Kardashian sisters wearing Black hairstyles (Kim wearing Fulani braids, Khloe wearing Bantu knots, Kylie wearing cornrows) are examples of cultural appropriation.

❖ **BEAUTY:** the appropriation of BIPOC physical features, such as thicker lips, rounder hips and thighs, darker skin (whether through tanning or wearing darker makeup). The Kardashians are another example of this.

❖ **SPIRITUALITY:** the appropriating of sacred BIPOC spiritual ceremonies, rituals, iconography, practices, and objects. Examples include white people leading "Native American" sweat lodges and vision quests, and white people being the predominant teachers of yoga in the West (while marginalizing South Asian people in these spaces).

❖ **WELLNESS:** the appropriation of BIPOC traditional wellness practices and healing modalities. This is especially present in the use of and profit from Indian ayurvedic practices and Traditional Chinese Medicine by people who don't come from these cultures.

❖ **MUSIC:** the appropriation of Black and American music styles, often filtered through a white lens (such as when rap music is used to make white artists look cool).

❖ **CULTURAL HOLIDAYS AND EVENTS:** the appropriation of costumes and characters from other cultures. Some cultural holidays and events use cultural appropriation as a main part of their celebration, for example Halloween costumes or the use of the blackface character Zwarte Piet or Black Pete in the Netherlands for the annual celebration of Sinterklaasavond (St. Nicholas's Eve).

❖ **LINGUISTIC STYLES:** the appropriation of AAVE or BVE by non-Black people. Examples include, *spilling the tea*, *throwing shade*, *shook*, *lit*, *yas*, *sis*, *snatched*, *bae*, *periodt*, and so on. You may think these are just popular terms, but they actually originate from Black culture. Many of the terms originate from Black LGBTQ communities, who face even greater discrimination.

The most harmful thing about cultural appropriation is that it seeks to use and exploit elements from a particular culture while actually continuing to marginalize and discriminate against people who belong to that culture.

How is it possible to appreciate

> **AAVE** stands for African American Vernacular English.
> **BVE** stands for Black Vernacular English.

a culture when we don't appreciate the people who created and represent that culture?

WHEN TRYING TO FIND OUT IF SOMETHING IS AN ACT OF CULTURAL APPROPRIATION OR AN ACT OF CULTURAL APPRECIATION, EXPLORE THE FOLLOWING QUESTIONS:

- What is the history that exists between my culture and that culture?
- What are some of the racist stereotypes and beliefs I have toward people of that culture?
- In what ways am I supporting, protecting, and uplifting people from that culture? (For example, if I love yoga, do I learn from South Asian teachers? Do I read more about the history of yoga from South Asian writers? Do I speak out against racism when it happens to South Asian people?)
- Do I understand the historic significance of sacredness of this cultural element to the culture? (For example, if I choose a Día de los Muertos costume for Halloween, do I understand the significance of this day in Mexican culture?)
- If I know something might be offensive to someone from that culture, why do I want to wear or use it?
- How can I direct any money gained from using that cultural element to people who belong to that culture? (Please note that paying to use a cultural element is not an excuse for cultural appropriation.)

WHY DO WE NEED TO LOOK AT CULTURAL APPROPRIATION?

You may be thinking *Colonialism was a thing of the past. Isn't cultural sharing a way to solve racism?* The answer to this is no.

Yes, colonialism in the way we have talked about it in this book is a thing of the past. However, other forms of colonialism do still exist, as do racist discrimination and violence, anti-Blackness, and racist stereotypes. Until these things are also in the past and there is no more dominance and nondominance/superiority and inferiority, we can't just call this cultural sharing. We have to talk about how cultural appropriation is used to uphold white supremacy.

Cultural appropriation upholds the white supremacist idea that white people can take whatever they want from Black and Brown people without consequence and that when a person with white privilege adopts something from a Black or Brown culture, they are somehow enhanced because it makes them look more exotic.

It's also harmful because it reduces people down to a racist stereotype and takes important aspects of their culture and uses them as costumes that can be put on and taken off. Cultures are not costumes. Black culture may be cool to adopt, but Black people have to deal with anti-Black racism and white supremacist violence. White people can put a costume of Blackness (like hairstyles, slang, or darker makeup) on or take it off, and they will never have to deal with anti-Black racism. When we take part in cultural appropriation, we ignore, minimize, and even contribute to the racist harm that other people experience.

RECAP, REFLECT, RESPOND

RECAP

Cultural appropriation is the act of taking or using something from another culture without the right to do so, because that cultural element does not belong to your culture. It often happens within a context of dominant and nondominant cultures and is used to enhance the person or company belonging to the dominant culture in some way.

REFLECT

❖ How have you or do you appropriate from other cultures?

❖ How have you witnessed white people appropriating from nonwhite cultures?

❖ Why do you think people appropriate from other cultures, even though they know it may be hurtful?

❖ What are some ways that we can show appreciation for other cultures without appropriating?

RESPOND

The question we should ask ourselves when thinking about cultural appropriation is not "*Can* I use this cultural element?" but rather "*Should* I use this cultural element?" Here are some ways to answer that question:

❖ Study the history between that culture and your culture. Is there a history of dominance and nondominance or marginalization?

❖ Understand the cultural or spiritual significance of that cultural element, and think about if it may be disrespectful for you to casually use something for your own entertainment that has deep significance for people from that culture.

❖ Think about how you intend to use that cultural element. Are you using it as a costume or for entertainment or clout, or are you using it in the way it was intended to be used?

❖ Ask yourself whether using that cultural element will contribute to fighting white supremacy or upholding it.

CHAPTER 16

white feminism

In 2016, British actress Emma Watson (a.k.a. Hermione Granger from the Harry Potter movies) founded a feminist book club called Our Shared Shelf. As part of her work as a UN Women Goodwill Ambassador, Watson was exploring books and essays about feminism and gender equality, and she wanted to provide a public forum where readers could discuss these books and learn together.

Watson chose the book *Why I'm No Longer Talking to White People About Race* by Black British writer Reni Eddo-Lodge as her first book for 2018. In her announcement letter for the book selection, Watson shared her experiences in the past with being called a "white feminist": "When I heard myself being called a 'white feminist' I didn't understand (I suppose I proved their case in point). What was the need to define me—or anyone else for that matter—as a feminist by race? What did this mean? Was I being called racist? Was the feminist movement more fractured than I understood? I began...panicking."

The same questions that Watson asked herself are the questions we are going to be exploring in this chapter: What is feminism? What is *white* feminism? What does white supremacy have to do with gender equality? And how can we make sure that all people of all genders, all races, and all identities and experiences are treated with equity and justice?

WHAT IS WHITE FEMINISM?

Before we dive into white feminism and its relationship to white supremacy, let's first start with some basic definitions.

WHAT IS FEMINISM?

- Feminism is broadly defined by Wikipedia as "a range of political movements, ideologies, and social movements that share a common goal: to define, establish, and achieve the political, economic, personal, and social equality of the genders." In short, feminism is about ensuring that all people of all genders are treated equally. It's not just about women's empowerment or girl power, but rather it's about making sure that everybody has equal rights, equal access, equal opportunities, and equal protections. White supremacy is inherently antifeminist because it is the opposite of equality for all people.

WHAT IS WHITE FEMINISM?

- Wikipedia defines white feminism as a term "used to describe feminist theories that focus on the struggles of white women without addressing distinct forms of oppression faced by ethnic minority women and women lacking other privileges."

In other words, white feminism focuses on the struggles of white women (usually cisgender and middle class) over BIPOC. It treats the feminist movement as one that is only about one thing—being female—and it ignores the fact that women and people who are BIPOC, who are poor, who have disabilities, who identity as LGBTQIA+ (lesbian, gay, bisexual, trans, queer, intersex, asexual, pansexual, two-spirit) and other marginalized identities also face additional struggles that take them further away from experiencing equality. Sadly, what we know as mainstream feminism is actually white feminism—an extension of white supremacy. White feminism does not include antiracism as part of its movement because it is only focused on gender (being female). Instead, it asks BIPOC to ignore their struggles with racism and only fight for their struggles with gender.

THIS REQUEST IGNORES TWO CRUCIAL POINTS:

1. White women do not have to consider the implications of their race, because they have white privilege. Race is not an identity where they experience oppression. Rather, it is an identity where they hold

power. To ask BIPOC to set aside their race is to ask BIPOC to act as if they are white.

2. To ask BIPOC to focus on gender before race is to ask them to put their different identities in hierarchical order. But as a Black woman, I am not Black *then* a woman. I am Black *and* a woman. My womanhood cannot erase my Blackness, and my Blackness cannot erase my womanhood. Under white supremacy, BIPOC women experience discrimination because of both our race *and* our gender simultaneously.

White women hold the expectation that Black women, Indigenous women, and women of color should stand in solidarity under the shared experience of gender discrimination, but as Mikki Kendall, the author of *Hood Feminism*'s viral hashtag, points out, #SolidarityIsForWhiteWomen. And white solidarity in the feminist movement is not a new phenomenon. The Western feminist movement has marginalized BIPOC from its very inception.

WHITE FEMINISM'S HISTORY

In the United States, the very first women's rights conference in Seneca Falls in 1848 failed to address the racism faced by Black women, Indigenous women, and women of color. In 1870, in response to the ratification of the Fifteenth Amendment, which secured voting rights for men of all races, Anna Howard Shaw, president of the National Woman Suffrage Association argued, "You have put the ballot in the hands of your black men, thus making them political superiors to white women. Never before in the history of the world have men made former slaves the political masters of their former mistresses!"

In 1913, before the first suffrage parade held in Washington, DC, suffragist Alice Paul wrote in response to the idea that white women and Black women march together, "As far as I can see, we must have a white procession, or a Negro procession, or no procession at all." And though white women received the right to vote in 1920 when the Nineteenth Amendment was ratified, because of racial discrimination, women of color in some parts of the United States were subject to many restrictions that made it almost impossible for them to vote until the 1965 Voting Rights Act was passed.

The feminist movement has, from its very beginning, been an extension of white supremacy. It has marginalized BIPOC and expected them to fit themselves into a so-called universal feminism that in reality centers white people. It is no wonder then that many Black women, Indigenous women, and women of color find it hard to see themselves in the feminist movement, opting instead for Black feminism, womanism, or no affiliation with the feminist movement at all.

WHITE FEMINISM TODAY

It is tempting to argue that these events were in the past and have no bearing on the current state of the feminist movement. However, white feminism and the divide between white women and women of color still exist. Just like white supremacy continues to thrive today despite the granting of civil rights, mainstream feminism continues to exclude and marginalize women of color. And despite white women experiencing discrimination and oppression under patriarchy, white women also enact discrimination and oppression against women of color under white supremacy.

> Patriarchy is defined by Wikipedia as
> "a social system in which men hold
> primary power and predominate in roles
> of political leadership, moral authority,
> social privilege, and control of property."

At the opening of this chapter, we read about the questions Emma Watson asked herself as she began to explore what being a "white feminist" means. She went on to share how her understanding evolved:

"It would have been more useful to spend the time asking myself questions like: What are the ways I have benefited from being white? In what ways do I support and uphold a system that is structurally racist? How do my race, class, and gender affect my perspective? There seemed to be many types of feminists and feminism. But instead of seeing these differences as divisive, I could have asked whether defining them was actually empowering and bringing about better understanding. But I didn't know to ask these questions."

Reading Reni Eddo-Lodge's book and the writings of other feminists of color helped Watson to understanding that what she thought was feminism was actually white feminism, and instead of being defensive about that, it was far more helpful to explore how her race, class, and gender impacted her practice of feminism. In other words, she began to learn about the importance of *intersectionality* in her feminism. More on this in a little while!

HOW DOES WHITE FEMINISM SHOW UP?

Here are some examples of white feminism in action:

❖ White feminists will talk about the pay gap between men and women without referencing the pay gap between white women and women of color.

❖ White feminists will tell women of color that talking about race is "divisive" and that we should focus first on being united under gender.

❖ White feminism largely ignores or is unaware of the way Black children are treated differently from white children (as explored in our chapter on anti-Blackness) and does little to address this difference.

❖ White feminism largely ignores and is unaware of the U.S. and UK Black maternal health crisis because it does not impact white women.

❖ White feminism largely ignores or excludes the groundbreaking works of Black feminist leaders such as Dr. Kimberlé Crenshaw, Audre Lorde, Dr. bell hooks, Alice Walker, Dr. Angela Davis, and other nonwhite feminists.

❖ White feminism does not believe Muslim feminists who choose to wear the hijab are real feminists.

The important thing to understand is that you do not have to be white to practice white feminism. If your feminism is only about gender and white ideas of empowerment and ignores race, class, disability, age, sexual orientation, gender identity, and so on, it is most likely white feminism.

WHY DO WE NEED TO LOOK AT WHITE FEMINISM?

White feminism is an extension of white supremacy. It asks Black women, Indigenous women, and women of color to ignore their race and focus only on their gender. During a speech at the Women's Convention in Akron, Ohio, in 1851, the African American abolitionist and women's rights activist Sojourner Truth said, "That man over there says that women need to be helped into carriages, and lifted over ditches, and to have the best place everywhere. Nobody ever helps me into carriages, or over mud-puddles, or gives me any best place! And ain't I a woman?" Sojourner Truth was asking if her Blackness made her less of a woman because she was not treated in the same way that white women were treated. And because of white supremacy, this still rings

true today. Under white feminism and white supremacy, the only way for women of color to be treated as
equals to white women would be to perform an impossi-
bility—to make ourselves white or raceless in the white
imagination.

The antidote to the poison of white feminism, and
by extension white supremacy, is intersectionality.

WHAT IS INTERSECTIONALITY?

Intersectionality is a term coined by law professor and civil
rights advocate Dr. Kimberlé Crenshaw. It is a framework
that helps us to explore how different identities and systems
of oppression are connected, particularly as they relate to
gender and race and the experiences of Black women.

Dr. Crenshaw helps us to understand that if you hold
multiple identities (like being Black and being a woman)
that are impacted by systems of oppression (like white
supremacy and patriarchy), then when you are experiencing oppression, it's likely to be because of both and
not just one or the other. She says, "Intersectionality
simply came from the idea that if you're standing in
the path of multiple forms of exclusion, you are likely
to get hit by both. These women are injured but when

the race ambulance and the gender ambulance arrive at the scene, they see women of color lying in the intersection and they say, 'Well, we can't figure out if this was just race or just sex discrimination. And unless they can show us which one it was, we can't help them.'"

Intersectionality gives us a way of practicing feminism that is antiracist. But intersectionality is not something that can be reached without a constant and unwavering commitment to antiracist practice. Using intersectionality allows us to see our whole selves and everybody else's whole selves too.

As Emma Watson shared, she began to understand that it was not just her experience of being a woman that was relevant but also her experience as a white woman with class privilege that informed where she had power and where she didn't. When we use intersectionality in our feminism, we no longer just fight for and with women broadly but also for and with women and people who are BIPOC, poor, disabled, LGBTQIA+, and more. This is what feminism is really supposed to be about—equity for *all* people.

RECAP, REFLECT, RESPOND

RECAP

White feminism is defined by Wikipedia as a term "used to describe feminist theories that focus on the struggles of white women without addressing distinct forms of oppression faced by ethnic minority women and women lacking other privileges."

REFLECT

❖ What was your understanding of the definition of feminism before you read this chapter? How do you understand it now, especially in the context of white feminism?

❖ If you identify as a feminist, to what extent do you think your definition was about gender only and not inclusive of race, class, disability, sexual orientation, gender identity, and more?

❖ How do you think practicing antiracism will help you to better practice feminism?

❖ How does understanding intersectionality help us to better fight for all people?

RESPOND

❖ When learning about feminism, try to learn from people from all backgrounds, not just straight, white, middle-class women. This will allow you to better understand how other people experience discrimination—not just as it relates to gender. Focus on keeping your feminist learning intersectional. A great place to start is the book *Read This to Get Smarter: About Race, Class, Gender, Disability, & More* by Blair Imani.

❖ If you are involved in movements, organizations, events, or groups that are about feminism and gender equality, use your voice to ensure that discussions and actions are intersectional. Also use these spaces to listen to the voices of BIPOC leaders.

❖ Share your learning with your friends and family! We are all constantly learning about ourselves and the world. The more we learn, the better we understand and the more inclusive can be our fight for equality and justice.

CHAPTER 17

allyship

My children, who were both born and have grown up in Qatar, attend the same British curriculum school that I graduated from. Despite being a British school, the student body is extremely diverse. During my years there, I remember that we had students from more than fifty different nationalities around the world. When we first moved to Qatar from the UK, I was in awe at meeting people from so many diverse backgrounds. I was no longer the "only." My cultural difference was just like every other student's, nearly all of whom were third-culture kids like me. It has been almost two decades since I graduated, and the student body seems to be even more diverse than when I was a student. And I am grateful that my children have had the experience of not being the only children of color in their class or school from day one of their education journey.

However, while the student body is wonderfully diverse, the teaching and leadership body is not. I cannot recall having a single teacher who was a Person of Color during my time there as a student, and while there are more teachers of color now, they are still the minority. At a parents' assembly a few years ago, I decided to raise this as an issue. I asked the school board and leadership why the teaching body was so white and what was being done to bring in more teachers of color. Separately, months earlier, I had raised an issue at another parents' assembly because I was unhappy that the reading curriculum for my daughter's grade featured novels from authors and fictional characters who were mainly white. In both cases, I received a sympathetic yet lukewarm response that they understood it was an issue and would see what they could do about it. They also shared that there had been efforts to bring in more teachers of color. But as a parent of the school, all

I had ever seen were a few token teachers of color, enough that they could say they were trying but not enough to come anywhere near to real diversity and inclusion.

I was left with the impression that they understood that it was a problem, but it was not a big enough problem for them. At the time, I felt that the most that would be done would be to add a few more token teachers of color and books by authors of color to satisfy the "look" of diversity without doing the deeper work needed for true inclusivity and representation. More recently, the school has begun its own journey toward antiracism, diversity, and inclusion, but there is still a long way to go.

Why is it important that my children have an inclusive mix of teachers to learn from? Isn't it enough that the student body is diverse? It's important because children and young people are impacted by who they see in positions of leadership and authority as well as who they see in fictional stories. I am also aware that unconscious racial bias and anti-Blackness from teachers with white privilege does not magically disappear because of a diverse student body.

The school's responses to my requests at the time

did not surprise me. Calls for greater inclusivity and representation from BIPOC are often met with similar responses, regardless of whether at school or at work.

In this case, I saw the school rely on tokenism as a way to prove that they were allies instead of them practicing true *allyship*.

WHAT IS ALLYSHIP?

You may have heard the terms *ally* and *allyship* during conversations about antiracism and supporting people who are marginalized because of their identities. Perhaps you've thought the aim of antiracism is to become an ally. People often use this word a lot without really understanding what it means. Additionally, people often think they are being allies through certain actions, while instead they are still maintaining the status quo.

In this chapter, we are going to explore what allyship is and isn't and how optical or performative allyship often gets in the way of authentic allyship.

A definition of allyship that I like to refer to is from PeerNetBC. They define allyship as:

"An active, consistent, and challenging practice of unlearning and reevaluating, in which a person of privilege seeks to work in solidarity with a marginalized group. Allyship is not an identity—it is a lifelong process of building relationships based on trust, consistency, and accountability with marginalized individuals and/or groups. Allyship is not self-defined—our work and our efforts must be recognized by the people we seek to ally ourselves with."

WHAT DOES THIS MEAN? LET'S BREAK IT DOWN!

♦ *"active, consistent, and challenging"*: It's *active*, meaning it's something we intentionally choose to do. It's *consistent*, meaning it is something we don't just do once in a while. It's *challenging*, meaning it should push us outside our comfort zone to really show up.

♦ *"unlearning and reevaluating"*: People often think that allyship is just about what you do to show you are not racist. But actually, a huge part of allyship is about unlearning and reevaluating what you thought you knew so that your actions can be informed by deeper understanding. For example, many people are better able to practice antiracism after they unlearn and reevaluate the idea that being color-blind is being antiracist.

- *"work in solidarity with a marginalized group"*: Solidarity means joining forces with a marginalized group to work *with them* toward the things that *they say* they need. It is not solidarity if you are working *by yourselves* on the things that *you think* they need. To work in solidarity with a group, you need to be listening to what they say and trying to help them achieve their stated goals for liberation.

- *"Allyship is not an identity"*: This is one of the biggest mistakes that people often make. They call themselves allies, thinking that an ally is something that you become. Actually, allyship is something that you do, not something that you are. It's a practice, not a label. It's a journey, not a destination.

- *"a lifelong process"*: Allyship is a lifelong journey where we are consistently and actively working in solidarity with marginalized groups. We never "arrive" at being an ally. Instead, we seek to live our lives doing our best to practice allyship.

- *"building relationships based on trust, consistency, and accountability"*: Allyship is all about our relationships with people. It's hard to work in solidarity with people who we have no relationships with—whether as friends, family members, community members, or team members. And those relationships need to be based on being trustworthy and showing up consistently and must involve accountability. Being accountable means being responsible for the things we say and do, whether helpful or hurtful. When we deny our hurtful actions, blame other people for them, or refuse to acknowledge or change our harmful behavior, we are not being trustworthy or accountable. (We'll discuss accountability in greater depth in the next chapter.)

◆ **"Allyship is not self-defined"**: Just like allyship is not an identity, it's also not self-defined. We don't get to say that we are being allies to a marginalized community. A white person cannot say they are being an ally to BIPOC. And actually, the goal isn't to try to be named an ally by BIPOC. Instead, the aim is to simply practice allyship as much as possible, using this definition.

WHAT ISN'T ALLYSHIP?

Now that we understand what allyship is, it's important to also understand what allyship isn't. Sometimes we think we are practicing true or authentic allyship, but actually it's optical or performative allyship.

Optical (meaning how something looks) or performative (meaning a performance or pretend act) allyship is when something looks like allyship but actually isn't because it doesn't meet the definition of allyship that we've discussed above. It looks impressive when you first look at it, but when you look a little closer, you can see that it's actually not really authentic. Let's explore more deeply what optical allyship looks like in practice.

> **OPTICAL ALLYSHIP** is a term coined by Latham Thomas in 2018. Thomas is an author, wellness leader, and the founder of Mama Glow, a premier maternity lifestyle brand. The terms *optical allyship* and *performative allyship* can be used interchangeably. For the remainder of this book, I will use the term optical allyship.

HOW DOES OPTICAL ALLYSHIP SHOW UP?

Because we now have a working definition of allyship, we now know that optical allyship is the opposite of authentic allyship.

OPTICAL ALLYSHIP

+ Isn't active, consistent, and challenging.
+ Doesn't involve unlearning and reevaluating.
+ Isn't about working in solidarity with a marginalized group.
+ Is about being an identity ("being an ally" instead of practicing allyship).
+ Isn't a lifelong process.
+ Doesn't involve building relationships based on trust, consistency, and accountability.
+ Is self-defined ("I am an ally").

A common way we see people practicing optical allyship is when they share a lot of social media posts about antiracism, but they don't actually practice antiracism in their real lives. The social media posts are easy to share (not challenging), make them look good to other people (about being an identity), and are sporadic (don't require building relationships based on trust, consistency, and accountability). The posts themselves are not harmful—in fact, they are helpful in spreading awareness and using their voice or uplifting the voices of BIPOC—but unless they are also supported by other acts of allyship, they are more about performing allyship rather than practicing it.

Similarly, we see optical allyship when people only want to show up for the fun and easy parts of allyship, for example wearing badges or taking part in viral challenges, but not for the more challenging work that puts them outside their comfort zone, like fundraising, community organizing, regularly meeting for relationship building, writing letters to demand change, attending marches, learning about antiracism, having challenging conversations with friends and family, and so on.

There are also two other main ways that optical allyship show up that are important to recognize: *tokenism* and *white saviorism*.

TOKENISM

Tokenism is defined by the *Oxford English Dictionary* as "the practice of making only a perfunctory or symbolic effort to do a particular thing, especially by recruiting a small number of people from underrepresented groups in order to give the appearance of sexual or racial equality within a workforce." At the beginning of this chapter, I shared how my children's school recruited a small number of teachers of color and includes on the curriculum a few books written by authors of color or featuring fictional characters of color. When a school, business, or community group employs or includes a small number of BIPOC to give the appearance of real diversity and inclusion, they are performing allyship through tokenism. Essentially, this small or "token" number of BIPOC are intended to represent all BIPOC or more BIPOC than they actually do.

THERE ARE FOUR TYPES OF TOKENISM THAT WE OFTEN SEE:

1. **BRAND TOKENISM:** When a predominantly white organization or event engages a few token BIPOC or uses BIPOC cultural elements to give the optical look of diversity while not actually being committed to inclusion or antiracism in practice or policy. They may use BIPOC on their websites, social media posts, or marketing posters or even have a few BIPOC in their employment or leadership. However, they do so to make the brand look like an ally rather than actually wanting to do the necessary work of authentic allyship.

2. **STORYTELLING TOKENISM:** When BIPOC characters are used on-screen to give the visual look of diversity or to supplement the main white characters. This type of tokenism is often seen in movies, on

television, and in books. BIPOC are often included as side characters rather than main characters.

3. **EMOTIONAL LABOR TOKENISM:** When people with white privilege or predominantly white organizations expect BIPOC to be the only ones to discuss and work on all matters related to racism. They expect BIPOC to carry the emotional burden of having to discuss racism and see them as experts on all things related to being a BIPOC. One example is expecting a Black class member to answer all questions related to what Black people think or how Black people feel.

4. **RELATIONAL TOKENISM:** When a person with white privilege has friends or family members who are BIPOC and uses these relationships to prove that they can't be racist. They might say "I can't be racist because my partner/children/cousins/best friends/teachers/favorite celebrities are BIPOC."

Tokenism is dehumanizing because it treats BIPOC as tokens (things) rather than people. BIPOC become "get-out-of-racism-free cards" that people with white privilege can use anytime to prove they are not racist and avoid the work of authentic allyship. It also deprives BIPOC of true representation. One of the reasons why the Marvel movie *Black Panther* was such an incredible success is because Black people so rarely get to see superheroes who look like them.

Tokenism is a great burden on BIPOC because it requires them to be the representative of all BIPOC, which is not fair or possible. White people have the privilege of being seen as individuals. They do not experience tokenism because they are seen as the norm and are never deprived of representation because of their race. They don't have to fear being used as the "token white person" to prove diversity and inclusion. BIPOC often don't have this privilege.

ASK YOURSELF
- How have you noticed tokenism being used in movies, TV shows, or books?
- If you are a BIPOC, have you ever felt you were being used as a token?
- If you have white privilege, have you ever used relational tokenism?

WHITE SAVIORISM

White saviorism is when people with white privilege try to "save" BIPOC from their supposed inferiority and helplessness, because they see themselves as superior in capability and intelligence.

BIPOC do not need to be saved. They are not less talented, creative, intelligent, or courageous than white people. In fact, having faced racism for many generations has required BIPOC to call on more of their talents, creativity, intelligence, and courage to find ways to survive and thrive despite racism. However, because white supremacy pushes the lie of white superiority, people with white privilege can sometimes find themselves thinking that allyship looks like rescuing BIPOC from their less privileged circumstances.

White saviorism can be seen in the voluntourism business, where well-intentioned white missionaries and volunteers travel to countries in Africa, Asia, and Latin America to "rescue" BIPOC from their country's poverty and lack of development. Though well meaning, such volunteers often travel to these countries with not much more than their passion and desire to do good. They do not pay much attention to understanding the historical background and cultural contexts that they are entering into. Instead, much emphasis is placed on the volunteers believing they have the right solutions to the country's issues without listening to and partnering with the people they intend to help. They are not working in solidarity; they are working in saviorism. Little focus is put on the impact that white supremacist colonialism has had on these countries and the issues they are currently facing. Additionally, many volunteers prefer to travel to these countries to support struggling BIPOC there instead of support-ing the BIPOC struggling in their own countries. The idea of being seen as a savior, hero, or messiah is very seductive. All it takes is a selfie or two with a Black or Brown child (often without parental consent, or with consent but without an understanding of how those photos are going to be used to paint a picture of white saviorism) to create this narrative. Allyship shouldn't be about making you look good.

White saviorism can also be seen in movies and fic-tional stories. Movies like *Pocahontas*, *The Greatest Showman*, and *Hidden Figures*, which are based on real people, have been reshaped to center a narrative of white saviors coming to the rescue of BIPOC. White actors in fictional movies like *The Help* play characters who have great emotional depth and nuance, while BIPOC characters are romanticized with racial stereotypes or oversimplified cultural contexts. The movie *The Great Wall*, in which actor Matt Damon is the main protagonist in a fictional Chinese story, is another prime example of white saviorism. In response to this movie, Asian American actress Constance Wu said, "We have to stop perpetuating the racist myth that only a white man can save the world. It's not based in actual fact. Our heroes don't look like Matt Damon."

White saviorism can also show up as teachers with white privilege wanting to rescue their students of color. It can show up as individuals and businesses hosting fundraisers and nonprofit projects to rescue BIPOC struggling against issues of lack of access and discrimination (rather than *partnering with* these communities in solidarity to fundraise or lead projects). And it can even show up as parents with white privilege wanting to adopt children of color (though this is obviously not always the case, it is something that parents should be aware of when wanting to adopt). In more subtle ways, white saviorism is people with white privilege speaking over or for BIPOC in the belief that they know better how to say what needs to be said.

ASK YOURSELF

- How have you noticed white saviorism used in movies, TV shows, or books?
- If are a BIPOC, have you ever felt like someone with white privilege was trying to "save" you?
- If you have white privilege, have you ever felt like you were trying to "save" BIPOC from racism?

WHY DO WE NEED TO LOOK AT ALLYSHIP AND OPTICAL ALLYSHIP?

The practice of antiracism is a practice of allyship. In order to practice anything authentically, we need to understand what it is as well as what it isn't. In fact, when it comes to allyship, understanding what it isn't is very important. When we understand why something that looks like allyship (such as tokenism and white saviorism) actually does more harm than good, we can make sure that our allyship is more helpful than harmful.

When we understand allyship and optical allyship, we can hold ourselves and other people accountable to do better so that we can truly show up as antiracist change makers.

RECAP, REFLECT, RESPOND

RECAP

Allyship is defined by PeerNetBC as "an active, consistent, and challenging practice of unlearning and reevaluating, in which a person of privilege seeks to work in solidarity with a marginalized group. Allyship is not an identity—it is a lifelong process of building relationships based on trust, consistency, and accountability with marginalized individuals and/or groups. Allyship is not self-defined—our work and our efforts must be recognized by the people we seek to ally ourselves with."

REFLECT

❖ Why do you think optical allyship is harmful?

❖ Why do you think people, schools, and businesses tend to practice more optical allyship than authentic allyship?

❖ Schools are a place of learning, but antiracism is just as much about unlearning as learning. What do you think unlearning means, and why is it important for people with white privilege to "unlearn and reevaluate" their understanding of race and racism?

❖ What are some ways that schools and businesses

can build real diversity and inclusion without using tokenism and white saviorism?

RESPOND

Allyship requires building relationships based on trust, consistency, and accountability. Make it a priority to build real, not tokenistic, relationships with BIPOC in your communities. A tokenistic relationship is one where you only want to be friends with that person because they are a BIPOC. A real relationship is when where you want to be friends with them because you share similar interests, hobbies, values, and experiences.

Now that you understand what authentic allyship requires, think about some ways that you can suggest your families, friends, schools, and clubs can practice authentic allyship.

HERE ARE SOME EXAMPLES OF THINGS YOU CAN ASK YOUR SCHOOL TO DO:

- ❖ Hire more BIPOC teachers and administrators.
- ❖ Stock more books by authors of color and featuring protagonists who are BIPOC (and not just books about racism!).

❖ Partner with BIPOC nonprofits and businesses in your communities.

❖ Ask the white teachers to read and work through the adult version of *Me and White Supremacy*, and suggest this Young Readers' Edition for a class read.

❖ Read more books about race, racism, and anti-racism in your classes. I've included a suggested reading list in the Resources section at the back of this book.

❖ Make changes to any school policies or practices that reinforce racist stereotypes or anti-Blackness.

CHAPTER 18

holding ourselves and others accountable

In the summer of 2021, nineteen-year old singer Billie Eilish was called out online for her past use of a racial slur against Asian people and mocking an Asian accent, which were caught on video. The video was recorded when she was around thirteen or fourteen years old and surfaced at a time when there was an increase in anti-Asian hate crimes during the coronavirus pandemic.

Many people called for Eilish to be "canceled" for her

racism, especially because she was also dating someone who had been known to make racist and homopho-
bic remarks. In response to the video, Eilish posted an
Instagram story to apologize, saying, "I am appalled and
embarrassed and want to barf that I ever mouthed along
to that word. This song was the only time I'd ever heard
that word as it was never used around me by anyone in
my family. Regardless of my ignorance and age at the
time, nothing excuses the fact that it was hurtful. And
for that I am sorry."

She went on to explain that the accent she used in
the video was not a mockery of anybody's accent but
rather a "silly gibberish made-up voice" that she "started
doing as a kid." Nonetheless, she also said, "Regardless
of how it was interpreted, I did not mean for any of my
actions to have caused hurt to others and it absolutely
breaks my heart that it is being labeled now in a way
that might cause pain to people hearing it."

Perhaps you heard about Eilish getting canceled?
Or you've seen or heard about other celebrities, people
online, or even people at your school getting canceled?
Everybody's talking about cancel culture, but when it
comes to practicing antiracism, what we really need is
accountability culture.

In this chapter, we are going to explore what it means to be *accountable* to ourselves and each other as we seek to create a better world.

WHAT IS ACCOUNTABILITY?

Accountability is about being responsible for our actions and the impact of our actions on other people (whether we intended them or not).

HOLDING OURSELVES ACCOUNTABLE

Often, learning to speak out about racism and calling other people out on their racist behaviors is relatively easy. What is harder, however, is learning to be accountable for our *own* behavior and *being compassionate with other people* when they make mistakes and missteps. It is easy to cancel people. It's far harder to *be* canceled and to make space for people who have caused harm to change their behavior.

> **CANCEL CULTURE** is defined by Wikipedia as "a modern form of ostracism in which someone is thrust out of social or professional circles—whether it be online, on social media, or in person. Those subject to this ostracism are said to have been 'cancelled.'"

In our last chapter, we explored the PeerNetBC definition of allyship as "a lifelong process of building relationships based on trust, consistency, and accountability with marginalized individuals and/or groups." Accountability is a key part of practicing allyship, because it is an important part of having healthy, authentic, and trusting relationships. Without accountability, we do not have to be responsible for anything we say or do and the harm that we may be causing (whether we meant to or not).

Imagine causing harm to your best friend (intentionally or unintentionally) but not taking responsibility and apologizing. How do you think your best friend will feel? And what do you think they will think about you and your friendship? Do you think they would still consider you their best friend? Or might they start to hang out with you less, because they don't feel as comfortable with you anymore and don't know if they can trust you to be a good friend?

That's how it is with allyship and accountability. In order to show up as allies for people who experience discrimination and marginalization, we have to be accountable for our own behaviors when we mess up and make mistakes that cause them harm.

And we *will* mess up!

As we've explored throughout this book, white supremacy behavior doesn't just look like name-calling or racist bullying. It is often more subtle, like tone policing, cultural appropriation, color blindness, and anti-Blackness. We are all capable of these things, whether we mean to do them or not.

Being human means we make mistakes all the time. And we live in a world where white supremacy and other forms of oppression like sexism, ableism, and other "isms" and "phobias" run rampant. If we're reading books like this, we are constantly unlearning these behaviors, learning new ways of being that are less harmful and more caring. It is normal to mess up and make mistakes. But it's also important to take responsibility for our actions when we do and be committed to being better allies in the future.

HOLDING OTHERS ACCOUNTABLE

In addition to holding ourselves accountable, it's also important to hold other people accountable. However, this is where things sometimes get more tricky, and instead of holding people accountable, we cancel them. Accountability and cancellation are not the same thing.

HOLDING OTHERS ACCOUNTABLE CAN LOOK LIKE THIS:

❖ Calling out or calling in people on their harmful behaviors

❖ Asking people to act according to their own stated values and commitments

❖ Engaging in dialogue for greater understanding, learning, and change

❖ Asking for apologies and amends to be made

❖ And if all else fails, choosing to no longer engage with that person (or if they are a celebrity or brand, no longer purchase their products or stop following them on social media)

BUT WHAT WE SEE AS MODERN-DAY CANCEL CULTURE OFTEN GOES BEYOND THIS AND INCLUDES THE FOLLOWING:

❖ Expecting people to be perfect and never mess up

❖ Not allowing for differing viewpoints and perspectives

❖ Bullying and personal attacks

❖ Willfully causing harm to the person being canceled

❖ Calling for that person to be ostracized from society forever

Cancel culture does not leave space for people to make mistakes, disagree, change, and transform their behavior. It simply asks that they be canceled, as if they never existed. While canceling someone may feel good or may feel like a form of justice, it leaves us with an uncompassionate world where change can never happen.

Please note, I am not talking about people who commit heinous crimes and show no remorse for their actions, and no desire to change who they are and what they've done. I am talking about the vast majority of us who mess up, see things differently, get things wrong, don't know better until we learn better, and want to do better but may not know the best way how.

Accountability is not about blame, shame, or punishment, toward ourselves or others. It's about taking ownership of and responsibility for our actions and the impact of our actions and asking others to do the same for themselves too. It is always easier to point the finger at what other people are doing wrong. But real leadership starts by looking at ourselves first and treating others the way we would like to be treated when we mess up, which we will.

Cancel culture cancels the *person*. Accountability culture asks the person to be accountable for their *behaviors*.

> Accountability
> is about what
> we do, not
> who we are.

Cancel culture leaves no room for mistakes. Accountability culture accepts that making mistakes is part of being human.

Cancel culture demands only one perspective. Accountability culture allows for differing perspectives while still demanding people be treated with dignity.

Cancel culture uses bullying and personal attacks as a way to find justice. Accountability culture uses ownership and compassion as a way to find justice.

It's not just that cancel culture is about being "mean" and accountability culture is about being "nice." Rather, it's that cancel culture asks us to treat each other as disposable, whereas accountability culture asks us to treat each other as redeemable. We do not need to practice antiracism by throwing ourselves or each other away. We can practice antiracism by calling out/in the harmful behaviors and then throwing ourselves and each other a life raft to find our way back to doing better.

HOW DOES ACCOUNTABILITY SHOW UP?

First, it's important to understand who we are accountable to.

We've already discussed that accountability is a key part of allyship and that in order to build authentic relationships with people who experience marginalization, we have to be accountable to them. We cannot say that we believe racism is wrong and then say or do nothing when we see racism happening to BIPOC around us.

But in addition to being accountable to BIPOC, we also have to be accountable to ourselves. In the final chapter of this book, we are going to explore what that looks like. But for now, remember that it's important for us to behave in line with our own values and commitments.

Second, it's important to understand who we are accountable for.

First and foremost, we are accountable for ourselves. We are the only ones who are fully accountable for our own thoughts, words, and actions. We cannot blame other people for things we have said and done or expect other people to not hold us accountable for ourselves. When we mess up, we must own it—whether or not we meant to cause harm. When we do not own it, we are effectively saying that we do not care if somebody was hurt by us. We must be accountable for ourselves as we practice antiracist allyship.

After ourselves, there are three groups of people we can hold accountable for their words and actions: our friends, our families, and our leaders.

OUR FRIENDS

Sometimes, our friends say and do things that are harmful to BIPOC. Perhaps they make racist jokes, take part in cultural appropriation, or even bully BIPOC. Confronting our friends can be difficult because we don't want them to be mad at us, and we don't want them to get upset or be offended—especially if they were doing something that they didn't know was harmful. But often, your friends are more likely to listen to you because they trust you and care about you.

When speaking to your friends about their behavior, it's helpful to speak to them privately, without judgment or attack, and with the intention to help them understand why what they are doing is harmful and how they can do better going forward. Instead of saying to them "That's racist! You're so racist!" you might instead want to use this approach.

SCENARIO:

Halloween is coming up, and your friend tells you they are planning their Halloween party costume. When you ask them what their costume is, they tell you they are coming as a Native Indian. They themselves are not Native Indian. They tell you they're going to order a costume online and ask you what you think. You understand that this is a form of cultural appropriation that is harmful and offensive to Indigenous people. You know that you have to hold your friend accountable for this and ask them to do better. Here's what you say:

"I'm so excited for Halloween and dressing up! I don't know if you realize this, but wearing a Native outfit for Halloween is actually harmful to Indigenous people, because it's using their sacred cultural clothes like play costumes. It's a type of cultural appropriation, which is racist, unfortunately. Most people don't realize that. In fact, I've just been learning about it recently, and I've been thinking about my own Halloween costume and how I can make sure not to be culturally appropriative this year. Maybe we can brainstorm some ideas together? I think we can come up with some creative ideas that don't cause offense to other people's cultures."

OUR FAMILIES

Holding our families accountable can also present its own challenges. Your family may not always want to listen to you if they see you as too young, but being young doesn't mean that your voice doesn't matter. Sometimes being young means you understand things a lot better than those who are older! Here's an example of how to use accountability in a family setting.

SCENARIO:

You're hanging out with your family at home, and somebody makes a racist joke. You find it offensive and want to have an accountability conversation with them. Here's what you say:

"I know you're only joking, but I find that joke offensive. I know that you're a kind and caring person, but that joke is actually unkind and uncaring because it uses racial stereotypes. I care about being kind and caring to people of all races, and when I hear you make a joke like that, it really hurts. I've been learning about racial stereotypes and how harmful they are, even when we're just making jokes. If you're open to it, I'd love to share what I've been learning about with you so you can understand why this is so important to me and why I hope you won't make a joke like that in the future."

OUR LEADERS

When I use the word *leaders*, I use it in a wide and general way to describe anyone who is in a position of leadership, influence, or power. This would include teachers and administrators at school, public figures, worship leaders, community leaders, and celebrities (actors, singers, comedians, YouTubers, social media influencers, and so on).

Whereas our friends and families know who we are, leaders and public figures do not usually know us personally. But we know them very well, and we can find ways to hold them accountable. Here's an example to show how.

SCENARIO:

Let's use the Billie Eilish example at the beginning of this chapter. Billie Eilish is called out for her past behavior that was racist to Asian people and hasn't yet apologized for it. Billie Eilish has no idea who you are, but you love her music. You decided to leave a comment on her Instagram:

"Hey Billie. I know you don't know me, but I'm a fan of your music. I saw the recent video of you that's been circulating online from when you were younger and you used an Asian racial slur. I don't know anything about the context of that video, but I do know that that word is offensive to Asian people and is racist. I was really shocked and saddened to hear you use it, and I know your Asian fans are really upset by it. I think it's important for you to take ownership for your actions and make an apology. I truly believe that you are a kind and caring person and will listen to the feedback you've been receiving about why that video is so hurtful. We all make mistakes, and we must own them when we do and say sorry. I'm trying my best to do the same too. I know it's hard to be called out, but please don't ignore the harm you've caused. None of us are perfect, but to ignore this would be worse than the harm caused by the actual video itself. I hope you'll apologize and make amends soon. Thank you for reading this comment."

WHAT IF THEY DON'T WANT TO BE ACCOUNTABLE?

Sometimes our friends, families, and leaders will refuse to engage with us about being accountable. They may try to shrug it off, laugh, ignore you, or get upset with you. They may refuse to listen to what you have to say and dig their heels in deeper. This can be really hard, but it doesn't mean that we shouldn't have these conversations. It also doesn't mean that we should simply cancel people. Everyone has the capacity to change for the better, even if that change doesn't happen immediately.

If you are a BIPOC, you don't have to beg people to not be racist. You don't have to beg them to see your humanity and treat you with dignity. But what you can do is show them that their behaviors are causing harm and ask them to do better. And what I want you to always remember is that whether they take accountability or not, you matter.

Holding ourselves and other people accountable is not easy. It's about having the courage to have difficult conversations, asking ourselves and others to take ownership for our behaviors, and trying our best not to cause the same harm going forward. It's awkward and uncomfortable, but it's worth it.

WHY DO WE NEED TO LOOK AT ACCOUNTABILITY?

Allyship without accountability is optical allyship. It's meaningless. We must not only say that we believe in practicing antiracism, but we also must follow through with our actions, and that means being responsible for our actions and asking other people to be responsible for their actions too.

As explained many times in this chapter, we are human, which means that we are going to mess up and make mistakes. We are going to cause harm and hurt people, whether we want to or not. Accountability gives us a way to repair what the hurt has caused and rebuild relationships based on trust. Accountability doesn't undo the harm that was caused, but it does provide a path toward healing, repairing, and finding a better way of being in community with one another.

Accountability is hard, which is why most of us avoid it. It's far easier to pretend we didn't cause harm and to cancel other people when they do. Accountability is not just about saying we're sorry. It's about truly listening, authentically acknowledging, sincerely apologizing, and really making amends and changing our behavior to do better.

Often, feeling embarrassed, ashamed, sad, guilty, angry, and misunderstood can get in the way of us being accountable. But remember, allyship is an active, consistent, and challenging practice of unlearning and reevaluating.

It's going to take work to change the world. And that's why we need each one of us showing up and holding ourselves and others accountable.

RECAP, REFLECT, RESPOND

RECAP

Accountability is about being responsible for our actions and the impact of our actions on other people (whether we intended them or not).

REFLECT

❖ What do you think is the difference between canceling people and holding people accountable?

❖ What do you think is the hardest part about holding ourselves and others accountable?

❖ How can we make it easier for ourselves to be accountable when we mess up?

❖ What are some unintentional harmful behaviors you can take accountability for today?

RESPOND

It is inevitable that we will, at some point, find ourselves in a situation where we need to take accountability. Here is what being accountable does and doesn't look like:

THE FIVE A'S OF BEING ACCOUNTABLE:

❖ *Accepting* the invitation to listen and sit with the uncomfortable feelings

❖ *Acknowledging* that we have caused harm by sharing how and why we did so (even if unintentionally)

❖ *Apologizing* sincerely for the impact of our actions

❖ *Amending* the situation by fixing the harm

❖ *Adjusting* our behavior based on the feedback we receive and the lessons we've learned going forward so we do not repeat the same actions in the future

THE FIVE A'S OF NOT BEING ACCOUNTABLE:

❖ *Avoiding* the invitation to listen and the uncomfortable feelings

❖ *Acting* like the victim who is being misunderstood or unnecessarily attacked, which means we never get a chance to reflect on how and why we may have caused harm

❖ *Accusing* others of causing harm to us or of not understanding our intentions

❖ *Absolving* ourselves of any responsibility to make amends

❖ *Abandoning* the situation entirely, never apologizing or taking responsibility for what we did

PART III

practicing antiracism

your antiracist
values and
commitments

We are at the finish line of this book! But certainly not the finish line of the lifelong work of antiracism.

Take a moment to check in with where you are at right now. How are you feeling? I imagine that you are experiencing a range of different emotions, from exhaustion and frustration to inspiration, determination, and more. Perhaps you have more questions than answers. That is normal. There's still so much more to understand about white supremacy, racism, and how we can practice antiracist allyship. The good news is that you are now far more equipped with knowledge and understanding than you were when we first started this journey! (To prove this, go back to the "What Do You Already Know?" questions in chapter 3 to see how your understanding has grown.) You are already so much further ahead to help change the world than you could ever realize.

Reading about and understanding antiracism is important, but even more important is making and keeping the commitment to practice antiracism for the rest of your life. In this chapter, we are going to prepare you to do just that by writing down your antiracist values and commitments.

Having clear and strong values and commitments helps us show up for the work of allyship with consistency and accountability, which are key for allyship. Our values remind us why we are practicing antiracism, and our commitments remind us how we are practicing antiracism. Each person's whys and hows will be different, and it's important that each of us get clear on what those are for us.

WHAT ARE VALUES?

Values are the principles and standards that guide how we live our lives and where we choose to use our time and energy. Our values are our personal sets of beliefs that determine our actions and what is most important to us in life. Our values are often a mixture of guiding principles we have chosen for ourselves and those that we have adopted from society and/or religion.

WHAT ARE COMMITMENTS?

Commitments are agreements or pledges to do something in the future.

CHOOSING YOUR ANTIRACIST VALUES

Below is a list of common values that can inform our whys. Take a look through the list and circle any that resonate for you. If you have a value that isn't on the list, add it!

Once you have your list, try and narrow it down to your top five values. These will be your top five antiracist values that remind you why you are doing this work.

* Leadership
* Respect
* Making a difference
* Freedom
* Love
* Kindness
* Honesty
* Authenticity
* Courage
* Empathy
* Resilience
* Dedication
* Passion
* Fairness
* Joy

- ❖ Learning and growing
- ❖ Being accountable
- ❖ Caring for others

MY TOP FIVE ANTIRACISM VALUES ARE LOVE, FREEDOM, MAKING A DIFFERENCE, AUTHENTICITY, AND COURAGE. What are yours? Write them down in your journal and refer back to them frequently to remind you why you are practicing antiracism.

CHOOSING YOUR ANTIRACIST COMMITMENTS

Commitments are not promises, because promises can be broken. Antiracism doesn't require you to be perfect and to not make mistakes. All it asks is for you to try your best and be accountable when things don't go the way you planned or hoped. Our commitments remind us of how we want to show up when we forget or get it wrong. Along with our values, they help us to get back on course and stay the course.

In your final journaling exercise for this journey, you are going to use the writing prompts below to create your own personal antiracism commitment statement. This is a written statement that you can keep in your journal, on your bedroom wall, on your refrigerator door, in the Notes app on your phone, or in a Google document. In fact, you can keep it anywhere and everywhere you want so that you can easily refer back to it anytime.

To craft this statement, think back on everything we have covered in this book. (This is where your journal comes in handy! Take your time to review your notes and answers to the questions from this book.) Think about what you are ready to commit to in your personal life, family life, friendships, and community life.

USE ANY OR ALL OF THE FOLLOWING WRITING PROMPTS TO HELP YOU CRAFT YOUR COMMITMENT STATEMENT:

❖ I am committed to showing up for this lifelong anti-racism work because...

❖ I am committed to challenging white fragility by...

❖ I am committed to using my voice for antiracism by...

❖ I am committed to challenging racism in people with white privilege by...

❖ I am committed to uplifting and supporting BIPOC by...

❖   I am committed to donating my time and/or money to the following BIPOC movements and causes...

❖   I am committed to continuing to learn more about antiracism by...

❖   I am committed to showing up even when I make mistakes by...

❖   I am committed to practicing accountability by...

Feel free to add any other commitment statements that resonate for you. And remember, this commitment statement doesn't have to be set in stone. It will change and grow as you change and grow. Come back to it as often as you like to rewrite it as you grow up.

YOUR ANTIRACIST AFFIRMATION

You may want to summarize your values and commitments into a single affirmation that helps you remember your values and commitments.

My own personal affirmation is *I am here to become a good ancestor.*

This statement reminds me that I am here to use my

gifts, skills, talents, and passions to help make a difference in the world and make the world a better place for the people who are here now and the people who will come after I am gone.

WHAT'S A STATEMENT THAT RESONATES FOR YOU? SEE BELOW FOR SOME EXAMPLES:

❖ I am here to change the world.

❖ I am here to make the world a better place for all people.

❖ I am here to lead with love and justice.

❖ I fight for freedom with courage, kindness, and empathy.

closing letter from the author

Dear Reader,

You made it!

After what has been an incredible journey, you have made it to the end of this book and the end of our time together. But the end of one journey signals the beginning of a new one, this time with *you* as your own guide as you seek to learn and unlearn more and grow as antiracist change maker.

You have learned so much on this journey: the history of European colonialism, the definitions of race, ethnicity, and nationality, the four different levels of racism, the different personal and interpersonal ways that white supremacy shows up, powerful ways to respond to this racism, and how to define your own personal antiracism values and commitments. You have really come a long way, and you should be very proud of yourself.

You've also learned something else that is perhaps of even greater importance, and that is the ability to *think critically*.

Critical thinking is the ability to reflect, analyze, question, theorize, and evaluate things from different perspectives. In each chapter, you have engaged in critical thinking by learning new information, asking questions, and providing your own answers. Critical thinking is key because it gives us the ability to not just accept what we are told as facts (like that Christopher Columbus "discovered" America) but rather to read and learn from different sources that give us a more nuanced and complex understanding of history and society.

It is my great hope that you will take this ability to think critically with you for the rest of your life and apply it to your journey of antiracist allyship. It's more than okay to question the things that other people (even adults!) tell you in order to seek deeper truths about how we can live in a fairer world.

As Octavia Butler, the late great science fiction author, wrote in her book *Parable of the Talents*:

"To shape God
With wisdom and forethought
To benefit your world,
Your people,
Your life.
Consider consequences.
Minimize harm.
Ask questions.
Seek answers.
Learn.
Teach."

Finally, to dismantle white supremacy—this system of oppression and discrimination that has hurt so many people for so many generations—we need all of us. In creating a fairer world, everyone's contribution matters. No matter who you are, you have the power to influence change in the world.

Using what you have learned in this book, start with yourself, your family, your friends, your school, and your community. The rest will follow as a ripple effect of your antiracist actions. You don't have to wait until you are an adult to change the world. You can start right now.

I hope you will. I know you will.

I believe in you, and I thank you.

Your friend and guide,

Layla

resources

glossary

AAVE: African American Vernacular English.

Accountability: Being accountable and responsible for our actions and the impact of our actions on other people (whether we intended them or not).

Allyship: PeerNetBC describes allyship as "an active, consistent, and challenging practice of unlearning and reevaluating, in which a person of privilege seeks to work in solidarity with a marginalized group. Allyship is not an identity—it is a lifelong process of building relationships based on trust, consistency, and accountability with marginalized individuals and/or groups. Allyship is not self-defined—our work and our efforts must be recognized by the people we seek to ally ourselves with."

Anti-Blackness: The specific racism that is experienced by Black people and people of African descent around the world. It is defined by Merriam-Webster as being opposed to or hostile toward Black people.

BIPOC: Black, Indigenous, People of Color.

Blackface: Wearing dark makeup to caricature a Black person. Its origins can be found in American minstrel shows of the nineteenth century where white actors wore dark face paint to depict racist caricatures of enslaved and free Black people on stage.

Cisgender: A term for people whose gender identity matches the biological sex they were assigned at birth.

Color Blindness: The idea that you do not see someone's color, that you do not notice differences in race, or if you do, that you do not treat people differently or oppress people based on those differences.

Colorism: A term coined by author Alice Walker in her book *In Search of Our Mothers' Gardens*. Walker defined colorism as the "prejudicial or preferential treatment of same-race people based solely on their color." Colorism is where prejudicial treatment is given to darker-skinned Black people and People of Color, and preferential treatment is given to lighter-skinned Black people and People of Color.

Cultural Appropriation: The act of taking or using something from another culture without the right to do so, because that cultural element does not belong to your culture. It often happens within a context of dominant and nondominant cultures and is used to enhance the person or company belonging to the dominant culture in some way.

Ethnicity: Refers to a grouping of humans based on shared social traits such as language, ancestry, history, place of origin, or culture. Examples of different ethnicities include Arab, Jewish, English, Dutch, Korean, Chinese, Nigerian, Tanzanian, Mexican, and Māori.

Exotification: The act of seeing someone or something from a different background or identity as being exotic, unusual, strange, mysterious, and "other." Racial exotification involves romanticizing different stereotypes about a different culture, and it arose from white, Western Europeans colonizing nonwhite cultures and countries.

Institutional Racism: This racism occurs *within institutions and systems of power*. This racism looks like unfair policies and discriminatory practices by institutions (such as schools, workplaces, and hospitals) that disadvantage BIPOC and advantage white people.

Internalized Racism: Also called personal racism, this racism lies *within individuals* and comprises our private beliefs and biases about race and racism, influenced by our culture. This can look like prejudice against people of a different race. For BIPOC, it can look like prejudice against oneself and other BIPOC. For white people, it can look like believing in the superiority of themselves and other white people.

Interpersonal Racism: This racism occurs *between individuals*. This is the racism that we see happening between people, whether in the classroom, on the playground, in public, or in the media. Tone policing (chapter 7) is a type of interpersonal racism.

Intersectionality: A term coined by law professor and civil rights advocate Dr. Kimberlé Crenshaw. It is a framework that helps us to explore the dynamic between coexisting identities and connected systems of oppression, particularly as it relates to gender and race in the experiences of Black women.

Misogynoir: A term coined by African American feminist scholar, writer, and activist Dr. Moya Bailey to describe misogyny directed specifically toward Black women. It is the intersection of sexism and anti-Black racism.

Nationality: Refers to your country of citizenship. It refers to the country on your passport or where you hold legal rights as a citizen. Examples of different nationalities include British, American, Kenyan, French, Australian, and Argentinian.

Optical Allyship: The visual illusion of allyship without the actual work of allyship. Also known as *performative allyship*.

Race: Refers to a grouping of humans based on shared observable, physical features, such as skin color, facial features, and hair textures. Examples of different races include Black, White, Asian, Native American, and others.

Racist Stereotypes: Negative depictions of wide groups of people who belong to one race or ethnicity. They reinforce the idea that these groups of people are inferior, other, and not civilized in the way white people are, with white people being the standard of what is considered "normal."

Structural Racism: Also called systemic racism, this racism occurs *among institutions and across society*. It involves many societal factors, like history, culture, ideology, and the interactions of institutions and policies that disadvantage BIPOC and privilege white people.

Third-Culture Kid: A person who was raised in a culture that is different from the culture of their parents and the culture of their country of nationality.

Tokenism: Defined by *Oxford Dictionaries* as "the practice of making only a perfunctory or symbolic effort to do a particular thing, especially by recruiting a small number of people from underrepresented groups in order to give the appearance of sexual or racial equality within a workforce."

Tone Policing: A tactic used by those who have (white) privilege to silence those who do not by focusing on the tone of what is being said rather than the actual content. Tone policing does not only have to be spoken out loud publicly. People with white privilege often tone police BIPOC in their thoughts or behind closed doors.

Voluntourism: The trend and business of volunteer tourism, where people with privilege from Western countries travel to do charity volunteer work in countries across Africa, Asia, and Latin America. Voluntourism has been criticized for perpetuating white saviorism.

White Exceptionalism: The belief that many people with white privilege often have about themselves that they are not racist, do not have racist thoughts, beliefs, or behaviors, and that they are "one of the good ones." This is the belief that other white people are racist but they aren't and that they are excluded from the effects, benefits, and conditioning of white supremacy, so they do not have to do antiracism work.

White Feminism: Defined by Wikipedia as a term that is "used to describe feminist theories that focus on the struggles of white women without addressing distinct forms of oppression faced by ethnic minority women and women lacking other privileges."

White Fragility: A term coined by Robin DiAngelo that is defined as "a state in which even a minimum amount of racial stress becomes intolerable, triggering a range of defensive moves." White fragility is the fight, flight, or freeze reaction that many people with white privilege often have when it comes to having conversations about racism.

White Privilege: A term that describes the unearned advantages, benefits, and immunities that white and white-passing people receive because of their race. Peggy McIntosh describes white privilege as "an invisible package of unearned assets that I can count on cashing in each day, but about which I was 'meant' to remain oblivious."

White Saviorism: Occurs when people with white privilege try to "save" BIPOC from their supposed inferiority and helplessness, because they see themselves as superior in capability and intelligence.

White Silence: Occurs when people who have white privilege stay complicitly silent when it comes to issues of race and racism.

White Superiority: The untrue and racist idea that people with white or white-passing skin are superior to and therefore deserve to dominate over people with black or brown skin.

White Supremacy: A racist ideology that is based on the belief that white people are superior to and better than people of other races and therefore they deserve to be dominant over and treated better than people of other races.

reading list

Interested in learning more about antiracism, activism, social justice, and changing the world? Here are some great nonfiction and fiction books written for young people to add to your reading list!

NONFICTION

* *This Book Is Anti-Racist: 20 Lessons on How to Wake Up, Take Action, and Do The Work* by Tiffany Jewell
* *Read This to Get Smarter: About Race, Class, Gender, Disability, & More* by Blair Imani
* *Road Map for Revolutionaries: Resistance,*

Activism, and Advocacy for All by Elisa Camhort Page, Carolyn Gerin, and Jamia Wilson

❖ *Black and British: A Short, Essential History* by David Olusoga

❖ *How I Resist: Activism and Hope for a New Generation* edited by Maureen Johnson

❖ *Youth to Power: Your Voice and How to Use It* by Jamie Margolin

❖ *This Book Is Feminist: An Intersectional Primer for Next-Gen Changemakers* by Jamia Wilson

❖ *Amazons, Abolitionists, and Activists: A Graphic History of Women's Fight for Their Rights* by Mikki Kendall and A. D'Amico

❖ *You Are Mighty: A Guide to Changing the World* by Caroline Paul

❖ *Black Girl, White School: Thriving, Surviving and No, You Can't Touch My Hair* edited by Olivia V. G. Clarke

❖ *Stamped: Racism, Antiracism, and You: A Remix of the National Book Award–winning Stamped from the Beginning* by Ibram X. Kendi and Jason Reynolds

❖ *An Indigenous Peoples' History of the United States for Young People (ReVisioning History for Young People)* adapted by Jean Mendoza, Debbie Reese, and Roxanne Dunbar-Ortiz

- *We Rise, We Resist, We Raise Our Voices* edited by Wade Hudson and Cheryl Willis Hudson
- *IntersectionAllies: We Make Room for All* by Chelsea Johnson, LaToya Council, Carolyn Choi, and Ashley Seil Smith
- *The Talk: Conversations about Race, Love & Truth* edited by Wade Hudson and Cheryl Willis Hudson
- *It's Trevor Noah: Born a Crime: Stories from a South African Childhood* by Trevor Noah
- *Marley Dias Gets It Done: And So Can You!* by Marley Dias
- *When They Call You a Terrorist (Young Adult Edition): A Story of Black Lives Matter and the Power to Change the World* by Patrisse Khan-Cullors and asha bandele
- *Just Mercy (Adapted for Young Adults): A True Story of the Fight for Justice* by Bryan Stevenson
- *Not My Idea: A Book About Whiteness* by Anastasia Higginbotham
- *Silence Is Not An Option: You Can Impact the World for Change* by Stuart Lawrence
- *The Secret Diary of a British Muslim Aged 13¾* by Tez Ilyas

- ❖ *What Is Race? Who Are Racists? Why Does Skin Colour Matter?* by Claire L. Heuchan and Nikesh Shukla
- ❖ *Coming to England 25th Anniversary Edition* by Floella Benjamin

FICTION

- ❖ *Watch Us Rise* by Renée Watson and Ellen Hagan
- ❖ *A Good Kind of Trouble* by Lisa Moore Ramee
- ❖ *We Are Not from Here* by Jenny Torres Sanchez
- ❖ *We Are Not Free* by Traci Chee
- ❖ *On the Come Up* by Angie Thomas
- ❖ *The Hate U Give* by Angie Thomas
- ❖ *Windrush Child* by Benjamin Zephaniah
- ❖ *The Place for Me: Stories About the Windrush Generation* by K. N. Chimbiri, E. L. Norry, and Judy Hepburn
- ❖ *Punching the Air* by Ibi Zoboi and Yusef Salaam
- ❖ *One of the Good Ones* by Maika Moulite and Maritza Moulite
- ❖ *I'm Not Dying with You Tonight* by Kimberly Jones and Gilly Segal
- ❖ *For Black Girls Like Me* by Mariama J. Lockington

- ❖ *Black Enough: Stories of Being Young & Black in America* edited by Ibi Zoboi
- ❖ *Woke: A Young Poet's Call to Justice* by Mahogany L. Browne, Elizabeth Acevedo, and Olivia Gatwood
- ❖ *Windrush Child* by Benjamin Zephaniah
- ❖ *Noughts and Crosses* by Malorie Blackman
- ❖ *Everyone Versus Racism: A Letter to Change the World* by Patrick Hutchinson

about the author

Layla F. Saad is an international bestselling author, speaker, and podcast host on the topics of race, identity, leadership, personal transformation, and social change. Layla is the author of the *New York Times* and *Sunday Times* bestselling antiracism education workbook, *Me and White Supremacy: Combat Racism, Change the World, and Become a Good Ancestor.*

As an East African, Arab, British, Black, Muslim

woman who was born in and grew up in the UK and currently lives in Qatar, Layla has always sat at a unique intersection of identities from which she is able to draw rich and intriguing perspectives. Layla's work is driven by her powerful desire to "become a good ancestor," to live and work in ways that leave a legacy of healing and liberation for those who will come after she is gone.

Layla's work has been brought into communities, workplaces, educational institutions, and events around the world that are seeking to create personal and collective change.

Find out more about Layla at laylafsaad.com.